First World Problems
101 Reasons Why The Terrorists Hate us

Ben Nesvig

THANKS AND STUFF

A special thanks to my wife for tolerating every awkward experience you're going to read about (and taking the book cover photo), to the guy I hired on Craigslist to edit this book, Luke for fixing what the guy from Craigslist missed, and to Kaia (http://www.exhibit-k.com) for designing the book cover.

Oh, and thank you for buying this book. Without you this book would technically still exist since publishing is free, but if you hadn't purchased this book, I wouldn't be well on my way to being able to afford a luxurious meal at Red Lobster.

CONTENTS

THE BEGINNING (OBVIOUSLY)

The "I'm Not a Horrible Person" Disclaimer

This book is 100% satire. Sure, it might be smushed full of nothing but good idea after good idea, but don't take it too seriously. Most won't, but I guarantee at least 1 negative review criticizing me as a horrible person for calling what follows "problems."

Everything that follows in this book/novel/prose/word vomit is pure opinion, except the part about my pillows being too fluffy. Hard to argue against that.

Read on. Or don't. But you've already bought the book, so don't be an idiot.

Who Am I?

Just a man with all of the worst problems in the world.

To avoid confusion while reading, here are some things you should know:

- At the time of writing this, I was anywhere between the ages of 24-25 years young.
- I was living with a friend from high school for half of the book. The other half I was engaged and now married.
- Lived in an apartment for a year.
- We moved on up to a house eventually (So much stuff to move).
- Had an old 1998 Chevy Lumina.
- Upgraded and bought a Kia Forte (What up!).

So when this book seems to have more flashbacks than Family Guy, it might be one of those reasons above. A lot has change in the two years I spent writing this book, but my problems only accrued.

Who Are You?

This is for you.

Yes, you reading this book probably on a Kindle or iPad.

I know who you are.

You're the unsung hero of your own world.

Day after day, the cold, cruel world beats its iron fist down on your dreams.

But you silently carry on.

I know your pain, your struggle, your silent fight to live in a better world where ice cream doesn't melt, buffets never close, and Costco never runs out of miniature wiener samples.

I know what it's like to drive while eating a giant melting ice cream cone. What it's like to buy so much food it molds. What it's like to burn your tongue on pizza because it's too damn hot and you're too damn hungry.

This is for you. I'm giving a voice to the voiceless. An anthem to the anthemless. A have for the have-mores.

I live in the First World and these are my problems.

What Are First World Problems?

It's likely you live a life full of First World Problems. Though, just like fish don't know they're in water, you may be completely oblivious because you're surrounded by them.

A First World Problem is a trivial issue that afflicts people in wealthier nations declared to be in the "First World."

First World Problem:
"We have nothing to drink in the fridge except water."

Third World Problem:
"I have to walk three miles to draw water from a dirty well or else I'll die of dehydration."

These problems are serious. The people are real. And the struggle is universal, unless of course you live in the Third World.

Everything that follows comes from personal experience.

FOOD / RESTAURANTS

A Prelude To Gluttony

Nothing has caused me more joy or pain in my brief existence on this planet than food - the mother of all First World Problems and the father of diarrhea. There is little need to explain why food is such a difficult problem for us - we have too much of it. Overeating to the point of near explosion at a buffet is as common as breathing.

We are swimming in a sea of obesity. It isn't pretty.

We didn't ask for it. And it's a large problem (Sorry to resort to a news reporter-level pun).

This is the grand opus to the massive American Masses, letting you know that you're not alone. This is the rallying belch. The victory lap around the buffet.

Unbutton your pants and dig in.

Bought Too Much Food and Now Everything Is Molding

The taste of wet sock dropped onto my tongue as I walked in the door of my apartment today. Either an elf farted and disappeared before I entered or more food has gone bad.

Deep within the annals of the refrigerator lay a brick of cheese that looked like it was being consumed by a swamp monster. Then into the vegetable container sat a perfectly good bag of lettuce. Except, it looked like soggy algae.

My eyes were bigger than my belly, which is rather impressive if you take a good, soft look at my belly. I'm not sure if it's a matter of buying too much or picking all the wrong stuff. The fruit I buy seems to have the lifespan of a mosquito. Some of the vegetables camouflage themselves the second I set them in the refrigerator. I can no longer see them until suddenly they are rotten.

The problem stems from wanting to show at least a little bit of a healthy conscious at the grocery store. It feels really good to buy carrots, celery, and the lot. Then when it comes time to actually eat something, it's pizza bagel bites by a mile.

And then there are the several issues I have with cashiers at grocery stores. I mostly shop at organic grocery stores where the check-out clerks are generally friendlier and a little too conversational. They will often comment on what I'm buying, which just makes me feel weird.

"Having pulled pork sandwiches tonight? That's awesome."

"Uh...yeah?"

Since the cashiers are constantly analyzing what I buy like they're playing a game of Clue, what are they thinking when they don't say anything? Especially during some of those questionable purchases that everyone has...

"Economy sized toilet paper, coffee, bottle of $3 wine, plunger, chips and dip...I'd like to solve the puzzle: We've got Ben in a basement bathroom with constipation from a cheese-heavy diet and an evening filled with unclogging a toilet and snacking while watching...The League. We'll see you next week!"

America should have saved the "Don't Ask. Don't Tell." policy for cashiers. We played that card too early. If anyone should be contractually bound to keep quiet, it should be cashiers seeing everything that you buy. I can't *not* buy mini frozen pizza bagels along with toilet paper on a weekly basis. There just doesn't need to be running commentary about it. Not now. Not ever.

We should rid the world of cashiers. Move everything to self checkout and it would solve all of our problems...

Couldn't Wait For My Frozen Pizza To Cool Down So I Burned My Tongue

I feel like a giant winner tonight. And why wouldn't I? My fat face was so hungry I couldn't wait two minutes for my $4 frozen pizza to cool down from 425 degrees.

After gracefully pulling the pizza from the oven, I had to shovel it in my mouth like a drug smuggler swallowing balloons of heroin.

It was a flaming mess, which left my roof raw and my modicum of self-esteem burnt to a crisp.

I'm not sure how I'll cope over the next couple of days. I might be forced to eat a couple of boxes of Ice Cream Sandwiches. Ice cream therapy is the only way my mouth will ever recover.

Hot food is superior to cold food, but you're far more likely to injure yourself with a hot cluster of food.

I know from experience.

In my short time on Earth I've burnt myself with French fries, Juicy Lucy burgers (cheese squirts like a fire hose), mozzarella sticks, cheese dip, cheese curds, bacon, bacon covered shrimp, bacon covered cocktail wieners, everything else bacon, and finally $4 frozen pizza.

It's a sad life, burning your tongue on frozen pizza, but it's my life.

Update: Four months after I originally wrote this, I yet again burned my tongue on two small frozen pizzas. After three ice cream sandwiches, the roof of my mouth is still tender. You can't teach an old dog new tricks and you can't get me to wait 45 seconds for my pizza to cool to a reasonable temperature. I'm not sure I have anything of value to contribute to society anymore.

The Biodegradable SunChips Bag Hurts My Ears

Meet the Vuvuzela of chip bags. This compostable bag makes it impossible to enjoy French Onion chips without waking the neighbors every time I reach for the bag. It's ridiculous. It's un-American. And worst of all, it almost keeps me from snacking.

How am I supposed to sneak a snack in the middle of the night? Are the makers of the bag trying to publicly shame me every time I want a little treat at 2am? Can a man not eat 1/2 a bag of chips without replicating the sound of a severe thunderstorm?

While you're at it SunChips, why not have someone follow me around point out every other flaw I have?

"This man doesn't wash his hands after using a public restroom."
"This man is wearing the same socks for the third day in a row."

Because at the moment, the deafening sound of the bag basically says: *"Everybody listen to this man eat the whole damn bag of chips. It's incredible. The gluttony. Hey neighborhood, it's 3am, can you believe he's still eating chips after that huge dinner and late night Taco Bell. What a chunk!"*

I get the intention behind the creation of the bag—to rid the Earth of pollution. But has anyone at the headquarters of SunChips ever heard of noise pollution? Because that is the real crime against humanity here. The Earth can take care of itself. It kind of has for a long time. My ears can only handle so many decibels of shame.

Until a man can eat 3/4ths a bag of Harvest Cheddar SunChips after a long day at the office without the audible indignity of a deafening bag, I shall find solace in Doritos. That is the type of crazy mixed up world we live in.

The solution here is fairly simple, but we just need to devote some of our best and brightest to it—silent chip bags. If we can make a silencer for A GUN, can we not do it for a mere bag of chips?

Currently, it would be more discrete for me to shoot someone with a double barrel shotgun than open a bag of chips. Think about the absurdity of that.

If we want our children and our children's children (don't care about further generations than that) to know America as America, we need to act swiftly in regulating chip bag noise.

For a better America.

Our Waiter Put An Uncomfortable Amount Of Effort Into The Specials Speech

Where is the orchestra? Our waiter's speech on specials is running into overtime and is still on the crescendo!

After our waiter returned with two cold beers, I couldn't take a sip before the prelude to boredom began.

"Tonight we have some very special specials for you."

"Yes, please let me know what food is expiring soon!"

"We've got a pan-seared mushroom glazed salmon…"

At this point I can't just chime in and say I hate mushrooms. They're slimy. Don't like slimy people or slimy food. If I did that, I could guarantee spit in my burger. 100%. Out of the goodness of my heart I don't deflate the sails of this young aspiring comedian, temporarily working as a waiter.

Another problem with the speech is that there is no heart in it. It's the manager's corporate-infused diatribe verbatim. The delivery of the specials comes off like the server is in a dimly lit cave, reading the ramblings of a terrorist group with an AK-47 pointed at him off camera.

My extensive experience listening to specials has helped me develop an extraordinary talent. I'm one of the best people in the world at feigning interest. If it was an Olympic sport, I'd make Michael Phelps' take-home medals look cute. Want to tell me specials at your restaurant? About your boyfriend problems? About how your cat did the silliest thing? I can look like the most interested person alive on the outside, while the projector inside my head is replaying an episode of Boy Meets World.

What would solve the "special" problem is an app on my phone that is a pocket orchestra, just like they have at all the award shows. I'd pull it out, crank it to full volume and cut him off as he says *"Would you like to hear?..."*

That'll do server. That'll do.

I Didn't Order My Pizza Online So I Can't Track It

While pressed for time, I hit #3 on speed dial and ordered a BBQ Chicken pizza faster than a man in sweatpants getting a 2nd plate at a buffet. While I was promised the reasonable time of 30-40 minutes for delivery, shortly after I hung up the phone I became concerned.

I had no idea what was happening with my pizza.

Over the past few months I have become so dependent on tracking my pizza online through Domino's Pizza Tracker. I know exactly where my pizza is at all times, from conception to birth and delivery. It must be the comfort an overbearing parent feels when their child is strapped with a GPS-enabled cell phone.

But now? Nothing. Is my pizza being made yet? Is it in the oven? Is it excited to see me? Does it know my name? Does it like watching Cheers reruns as much as I do? Is it wearing a seatbelt in the car? Is it thirsty? Does it like to sing in the shower? Dance like no one is watching? Love like it has never been hurt?

To those questions I have no answer. Instead I'm worrying it will never find me, like a senior citizen who fell down without Life-Alert.

God speed, pizza. I don't even know you, but I can't wait to meet you.

Our Server Brought Out The Dinner Plates Too Early Causing False Excitement

Dinner plates are the foreplay of the meal at every restaurant. It's a signal that says *"Giddy up. Loosen the belt. Brace your arteries. And prepare to shovel down fried food."*

Tonight, our waitress in an unforgivable act, brought out our dinner plates and silverware unreasonably early. I found myself checking the time on my new iPhone repeatedly, wondering if I would ever know the taste of half-price appetizers again.

Bursting through the double swinging doors jaunted a short, unshaven man carrying a tray filled with several fine dishes of delectable mozzarella sticks.

Dinner had finally arrived. I could interrupt Angry Birds and nodding in agreement to whatever my wife was saying.

The cold breeze of the server blowing by my table to the ungrateful couple next to us left an emotional scar. I could have sworn he glanced at me like *"Hey, buddy. These are hot and ready, just for you, pal."*

But, no. The table with two kids in high school, probably on the first date, get my mozzarella sticks. The guy barely weighs a buck fifty. There is no way they're going to eat all of that food. Those poor mozzarella sticks.

I'm convinced this is all a ruse so I'll drink my beer quicker and have to order another drink. I'm no conspiracy theorist, but you don't have to be one to see something this obvious.

After what felt like 3 hours, but was actually 45 seconds to a minute, out came our mozzarella sticks.

No man should be teased with cheese like that.

The Coldstone Creamery Employee Didn't Sing With Enthusiasm

It's the little things in life that seem to make everything tolerable.

One thing I like to do when I feel a little morose is visit Coldstone Creamery—say about 2pm in the afternoon when no one is there. It's too late for lunch and too early for an afternoon snack.

Today I strolled into Coldstone by myself to get the Like-It Birthday Cake Remix. The indifferent employee began mashing the ingredients like a frustrated toddler pounding Play-Doh.

Then the magic happened.

The young man looked up at me to hand off the ice cream and I dropped a Washington into the tip jar.

Dance, monkey, dance!

I gave a little shrug implying an "*Eh?*" as in, warm up the vocal chords. Charles (he probably goes by Charlie, though) looked at me like I just pooped on his pillow. After a soft sigh, he began his rendition of "We wish you a Merry Christmas" substituted with Coldstone lyrics. There wasn't much heart in it.

Here is my problem with this: If you're not going to give 100%, don't bother doing it. I give 100% to the rush hour audience who hears my rendition of Jean Valjean from Les Miserables. I don't put out a tip jar though. When you work at Coldstone, if you're not a cabaret nerd, what are you doing there? At least show some passion in what you do. Lord knows we never have enough awful people singing in America.

The Server Took My Food Before I Was Done Eating

While out dining with the Mrs, I ordered a massive cheese curd burger and sweet potato fries with bacon seasoning. Yes, that exists. Now, I'm not normally one for your basic freedom fries, but these were kind of amazing.

We might have also ordered a few appetizers at the same time. Hard not to when the Happy Hour is amazing.

The food came in one fell swoop and I savagely ripped into the burger like a hyena post-kill on Planet Earth.

The table became a mess and I went to the men's room to wash up. When I sat back down, the server came over and asked, "Are you done here?"

This is a loaded question.

She wants me to say "Yes," so she can bring the bill and move onto the next customer.

The table looked like someone laid down a tray of food and dropped a grenade on top. It was a disgusting delicious mess, but I wasn't finished.

"Yeah…yeah, I'm done."

I wasn't done. I'll never be done. Another night where I'm forced to stop for ice cream on the way home.

It Is Impossible To Get Light Mayonnaise On A Sandwich

Hey, entrepreneurs! Do me a favor and invent a deli that knows how to put a reasonable amount of mayonnaise on a sandwich. No such place currently exists. It's impossible to get a decent spread of mayonnaise on a sandwich.

Today, I ordered a club sandwich with a dusting of mayo. What I received was an eye roll and splattered on mayo that sounded like a Green Bay Packers Fan farting on the way home from a brunch buffet. Yummy.

I do have a running conspiracy theory that can't be disproved. It might be even be on the deleted scenes in the movie Conspiracy Theory or The Informant.

Theory: Restaurant managers instruct their staff to plaster on a comical amount of mayo like the icing on sheet cake from a grocery store. Disgusting splatter by splatter, the consumer gets fatter until they eventually demand MOAR MAYONNAISE! They're willing to take a small loss in the short term, to make you fatter and hungrier in the long run. Brilliant.

It's insane. Does no one else care? Where are the big wigs in Washington on this? Probably wiping the mayonnaise off their dirty hands with Benjamins.

Side note - Why do so few sandwich places have avocado? It's the Cadillac of condiments. Your worth as a sandwich welder should be judged by your ability to appropriately stock avocado. Instead, we keep getting a fire hose of mayo pumped down our throats.

Ordered Eight 25 Cent Wings and Received Six

Outrage. Shock. Depression. Regret. Shame.

It's a whirlwind of emotions right now. My vision is blurry and I'm struggling to pen each key stroke to vent this travesty that happened tonight.

For Monday Night Football I decided to go to a bar that has free beer and 25 cent wings for the first quarter. Sounds great, right? I order my free beer and 8 buffalo wings. (I didn't order 12 since I had a light dinner and ordering 6 would be too emasculating.) Moments later, the waitress returned with the beer and my wings. She trotted back to the kitchen as I prepared to strip the meat from the wings like a hyena.

I looked at my plate of wings...

No...no!...what is this?...surely she can't be serious?...is this a joke?...

6 pitiful wings when I clearly ordered 8. By this point the waitress is deep inside the kitchen complaining to the cook about her boyfriend while I am in a Mexican Standoff.

Do I call her back to the table to let her know my fat keister didn't get the correct amount of 25 cent wings? Do I let this injustice passively pass me by? Do I take 50 cents out of my sad tip on the $2 bill.

In a perfect world, I would have been able to correct this error.

"Madam, pardon me, but it appears you may have had a slight in the tally of my wings. Respectfully, our agreement was to receive 8 of your finest wings, but I do declare that I only received 6. What do you say we make this right, darlin'? Ta ta."

But today this would translate into *"Hey butthole, I ordered 8 wings and I only see 6. Yeah, I know I'm drinking free beer and the wings are only 25cents a piece and I probably should have ordered 6 or 12, but my chunky tush wants those 2 wings. Pronto tonto."*

Were I to correct this server, I would come off like an old man complaining that his ice cream is too cold on a hot day. This is the state of affairs in America today. Shame over being labeled as a cheap schmuck. It's why I want to vomit every time I show a restaurant a Groupon. The inability to look cheap caused the housing crisis and it is now responsible for the much more serious wing crisis of 2012.

What did I end up doing? Tail between my legs I sat tight lipped, humiliated, and disappointed that the social mores of our society couldn't rectify this monstrosity.

One day I will see justice served – and dammit, it will be a full portion.

Girl Scout Cookies Box Has Less Cookies Than I Remember

I know it's a recession, but come on! Cut my pay, raise gas prices, inflate the dollar, make me work the weekend, but how dare you cut back on the standard amount of Girl Scout cookies per box?

My Tag Alongs barely have cookies to tag along with. Thin mints are anorexic. The Somoas are only some. And I've been shorted on the short bread cookies.

In life you expect some constants: death, taxes, and the outstanding American Girl Scout Cookies. Yet, this year the size of the box was the same, but the spacing between the cookies was slightly wider so there were less cookies per box. It was like subtly being given back less change from a cashier and not noticing it until you're already home.

Don't think for a minute that this means that I'll be eating less cookies this year. The exact opposite. I'll have to spend more money and double down on cookies. Probably buy a box of every kind except trefoils since those are for people who were born without taste buds. It's a disgusting cookie. Trefoils—makes you think of eating a tree wrapped in tin foil.

Eating 2x the cookies won't be easy, but dammit I've got no choice. Because asking me to eat less is unreasonable and no where in the constitution does it say I need to. The President may say we need to tighten our belts, but that doesn't mean I can't just buy a bigger belt to tighten.

You win Girl Scouts. You win. You invented a cookie I can't live without and then forced me to buy more of them.

It all makes sense why the cookie monster became a monster. Repeated cookie gouging could make any man a monster.

Enjoy your windfall profits, girls.

Mcdonald's Made Me Feel Like a Jerk For Not Donating Money

I'm the worst person in the world, - or so McDonald's makes me feel.

To start, I'm not proud of going to McDonald's. It's almost on par with a strip club or sex shop. Anonymity is king. You want to get in and out. Be neither seen nor heard. That's why when I get to the drive through window, I want to place my order and move on as quickly as possible.

And today I'm the worst person in the world.

I already feel bad about what I'm doing, - and then McDonald's makes me feel like I pooped the bed at the slumber party.

After I placed my order, the cashier asked, *"Would you like to donate a dollar to some children's fund?"* Ugh. You see, it's not that I'm against giving money to charity. I'm not at all. Part of the proceeds from this book will go to a charity. It's just that I want to know about the charity before I donate. Today, anyone with a box of band aids calls themselves a charity.

Charities can be shadier than a palm tree at high noon. Before I give a dime to a charity, I want to know how they will use the money and how much they spend on overhead. For all I know, they could be funding Libyan drug lords. I couldn't sleep a full 8 hours on my Sleep Number Mattress knowing that.

But it's impossible to not feel like a jerk in this instance. I just spent $7 on gluttonous fast food for myself and I can't spare a single dollar for a poor kid who just wants to make his short time on this earth tolerable?

I'm a horrible person. Thanks for the reminder, McDonald's.

I Didn't Order What I Wanted At An Italian Restaurant Because I Couldn't Pronounce The Name

This is a crime against humanity. Italian restaurants were invented to make Scandinavians feel dumb. I have no idea how to pronounce half of the menu. Delicious food available only if you're willing to look like the kid who gets called on to read in 8th grade and can't annunciate for squat.

There are a few ways you can subtly avoid looking like an idiot, but out of spite I won't do it.

1. You can mumble the part you can't pronounce.

2. You do the casual point to the menu, which makes it look like you have the memory of a goldfish.

3. You can get the unlimited soup and salad like a chump. And lastly, (which is my favorite) you only say part of the item. I end up saying "I'll get the Sicilian…" and just hope the server picks up on the rest.

If we want to make things easier on everyone, the names of items at exotic restaurants (Olive Garden, Don Pablos, Taco Bell, etc.) should have the phonetic spelling in brackets next to the name, just like the dictionary. As a society we are forcing restaurants to show the calorie count, when we should be forcing them to let us know how to pronounce all of the delectable items.

It's all I want. How am I supposed to know if two L's in a row make an "L" sound or magically transform to a "Y" like in quesadilla?

This is why I can't eat at nice restaurants.

Accidentally Bit Into a Raisin Cookie Thinking It Was Chocolate

Today, when I was nearing a state of exhaustion from not having snacked in at least 45 minutes, I stumbled upon gold - chocolate chunk cookies. The '95 Chicago Bulls of Cookies.

Without a second of hesitation, I grabbed the biggest one out of the bag and cookie monstered it. That soft dough, the crunchy oatmeal, the chewy...WTF!!! Raisins!

The raisin just piggy backs off the deliciousness of chocolate. It's like a bad movie sequel with none of the original cast. Do people really order raisin cookies (retirement home and Kindergarten classrooms excluded)? The only people who enjoy them are people who simply don't know any better—kids and senior citizens.

Raisins have no business being anywhere near a cookie. They're only good in cereal or when smothered in chocolate. Before anyone would ever eat a plain raisin they have to tell themselves a story like, "Getting a great form of iron here." When you have to verbally justify what you're eating, you know it's gross.

Raisins are past their point of being useful. They're wrinkled, dry, and seem to appear lost wherever they turn up. Actually, they are very similar to the elderly.

I ended up reluctantly chewing the gooey bite and pawning off the cookie to the dog. Such an unfortunate waste of cookie dough.

Sweet Martha would be sad.

Found a Seed In My Seedless Watermelon

Hello needle, meet haystack.

I had a crazy assumption today that my seedless watermelon would be...seedless!

Wrong!

The seed in the seedless watermelon is like finding a green olive in your pepperoni pizza. It doesn't belong there, but you just have to tolerate it.

Calling them seedless watermelons is rarely accurate. But you can't call them "Watermelons with a few scattered seeds."

Luckily for the watermelon company, I've mostly rid myself of the phobia of swallowing a watermelon seed and having watermelons grow in my stomach. Now I mostly just have lingering doubts, but I'm almost over it.

I should be blaming my lack of a butler. If I had someone like Geoffrey from the Fresh Prince of Belair to check my watermelons for seeds, I'd be living large.

Instead, I have problem after problem, sandwiched between more problems and more sandwiches. I'm such an optimist this might be one problem I can spin a positive on. I'm one of the best seed spitters this side of the Rockies. Give me an average watermelon seed and I could knock the cap off Abe Lincoln from 15 yards.

When it comes down to it, all I want is my seedless watermelon to be seedless. Society needs to demand better of our farmers. We wouldn't accept "Birth Mostly in Control." Why should we take "Just a couple of seeds, seedless watermelon."

Give me watermelons without seeds! Or don't and I'll quietly complain about it.

Bought Too Big Of An Ice Cream Cone And It's Dripping On Me

A beautiful summer day slowly collapsing at the hand of a dripping ice cream cone...Like one of the glaciers in an Al Gore documentary, my ice cream cone is disappearing rapidly at the ruthless tyranny of the sun.

Ice cream parlors are unpredictable. A scoop is the most relative thing on planet earth. To one parlor it's a golf ball, to another it's a regulation-sized WNBA ball. The only barometer you have is the person in front of you.

The only person in front of me today was a small kid. I didn't realize that scoops were adjusted depending on your age and height. He ordered two scoops, which didn't amount to much, so I ordered three scoops with a chocolate-dipped waffle cone, respectively.

The man behind the counter handed me his recreation of the leaning tower of Pisa, like I was the host of Man vs Food. Three softballs piled on top of each other with a slight lean to the left.

The second I stepped outside, the ice cream cone made a full charge toward my hand like an avalanche on crack. What felt like a side show novelty act, I continuously spun the cone like a plate, desperately trying to keep the ice cream from touching my hand.

Was I successful? No. No, I wasn't. I received a nice milky ice cream hand-bath. Absolutely delicious to lick up, but it should have never happened. Plus, now my giant stomach is upset since I ate the ice cream so quickly.

If the ice cream is too frozen, you'll get a headache. If it's too soft, it'll melt all over you.

There are no winners in the Summer ice cream eating game.

I Look Like An Idiot When Eating Popcorn

Popcorn is a conflicting snack. It's absolutely delicious, especially from a gourmet popcorn place. But it's also hard to really establish self-control. When I visit a place that specializes in premium popcorn, bet the house on me emptying my wallet.

When eating popcorn, you have the inevitability of looking like an idiot. If you eat popcorn and really enjoy it, and by that I mean that you don't go kernel by kernel but shovel by shovel, you'll look like damn fool.

Popcorn is the violin of snacks. Beautiful, but could take a lifetime to master.

It's impossible to eat popcorn without looking like a raging, starving idiot. You end up grabbing a giant handful with kernels spilling out before you can get your hand out of the bag. Then, if you only eat part of the handful there is a 100% chance you'll spill a few more kernels on yourself. It's humiliating, like your shirt needs gutters to catch all of it. You're lucky if any popcorn makes it into your pie hole.

Popcorn is the only snack where it is certain that 50% of it will end up in your lap or on the floor. If it weren't so delicious I'd have passed on it a long time ago, but butter is the nicotine of food. Put it in anything and people will beat down your door to get it. It's the only reason people in America eat bread.

It's the toll I pay, looking like a chotch while smushing popcorn into my mouth. In my Utopia, I would be able to eat popcorn like the people on Dateline who wish to remain anonymous and blacked out. When you look at me, you would just see a blacked out face while hearing the crunching popcorn, sounding fondly reminiscent of a trash compactor.

Just once I'd like to eat popcorn without people looking at me with the disdain of a nose-picker.

Ate Just a Few Handfuls Of Cheese Popcorn And Now My Hands Are Orange

Today, I had the fleeting thought that cheese popcorn would make a great snack at work. To the surprise of my double chin, it was a terrible idea.

Cheese popcorn is one delicious enigma. It's clearly the best popcorn on the planet, or at least until someone invents bacon buttered popcorn. But with that sweet sin, you've also got your scarlet letter—stained orange hands.

I'm like a modern day King Midas. Except instead of painting a town gold I've cheesed myself, everywhere.

Taking a child's handful of popcorn results in hands that will turn anything you touch to cheese. It's impossible to get any work done, unless I want to get cheese all over the keyboard like a freak.

So I retreat to an area where no one will find me and silently suck the cheese off my golden fingers.

The only problem I have with cheese popcorn happens when you eat it in public. In private, you can force it down like you're trying to repack a sleeping bag. Then, when the damage has been done you suck on your fingers like some sort of weird fetish flick.

It's too bad licking the cheese off your fingers is stigmatized in America. In today's hustle and bustle world, who has the time and especially energy to walk to the bathroom and give a "doctor going into surgery hand-washing" to rid themselves of the gluttony?

Billion Dollar Idea: Stainless Cheese Popcorn. Never again will I have to say, "Sorry, I probably shouldn't shake your hand Senator. I just ate bags of cheese popcorn."

Make it happen Zuckerberg.

Our Hibachi Chef Wasn't Asian

Call me old fashioned, but I like some authenticity when I go out to eat. When I go to Chipotle, I like to see Mexicans working there. When I go to a gym, I like everyone working there to be in shape. At a Chinese restaurant, I want my server to have a giant Chinese accent. The bigger the accent, the better the food. When I go into Old Country Buffet and I want to see an ocean of sweatpants. And of course, when I venture out to a hibachi and teppanyaki establishment I want someone of Asian descent preparing my meal.

The Asian man may be of no greater skill level than a Caucasian or Mexican, but it makes you feel good. Like when your parents checked your closet for monsters as a kid. They weren't actually doing anything, but it felt great. If you ask the audience on Family Feud, "Who makes a better sushi roll: Jose or Wong?" Wong wins 100/100. Game over, Louie.

Tonight, our chef in charge, Jose, timidly graced the table and began the pitiable show. To his credit, it had to have been his first night. Part of me felt like I should tell him to take a hard 5 and I could take over the throwing shrimp tails way over my giant hat into the next table act. I kept thinking he must be an understudy chef. Wong must be sick with the whooping cough or some ravaging disease.

The one saving grace Jose had, his ace of spades, was the onion train. Everyone has seen the chef make steam come out of the onion volcano, but Jose took it a step further. He let the table know that although he has been off his game the entire night, he can still throw a 95mph fastball right down the pipe.

Jose arranged the onion tower, poured in whatever makes the steam, and suddenly brought up zucchini as the caboose of a train. In what can only be explained as downright adorable, he pushed along the train and chirped a few "Choo, Choos." Precious.

Well done, Jose. For that very small moment in time, I didn't care that you weren't Asian and I felt confident about my meal.

Unfortunately, later in the meal when you tried to spin an egg with the crushing grace of Andre the Giant, I forgot all about the cute onion train.

Note to all Asian restaurants: Just give all of your employees Asian names. No one has the plums to question their authenticity and it'd help me sleep at night.

Accidentally Farted While Driving With My Mother-In-Law In The Car

I've lost sleep over whether or not I should take this story to the grave with me. After tossing and turning, some nachos, and a pint of ice cream, I've decided it would be selfish not to share. Please learn from this.

While driving from Nebraska to Minnesota with my Mother-In-Law and wife, we stopped for some lunch at a greasy hole in the wall in Anytown, USA. The food was on par with an elegant gas station's offerings, but I had to eat all of it since I would feel bad wasting food when not picking up the bill.

Back on the road, with my Mother-In-Law driving, wife in the front seat, and myself casually reading in the back seat. Nothing but the open road and books to read.

And stomach pain.

It felt like a little gremlin was inside me, trying to wring out my intestines like a wet sponge. Five minutes of this and I was about to explode through the roof of the car like a fighter pilot hitting the eject button.

I'm a logical gas man. We were in the middle of nowhere. The fans were blowing air past me. And I had a buffer of 3 feet from my wife and mother-in-law.

So, I let a little bit of steam loose.

Huge mistake.

Potency *always* trumps quantity.

Frantically, I began trying to sniff up the egg fart. While desperately trying to recycle the air and huffing like a fat kid hitting the last step of a flight of stairs, my wife outed me.

"Ewwwww, Ben! Gross!"

Game over. I fouled the nostrils of my Mother-In-Law and tarnished my name and reputation. But then my Mother-In-Law commented:

"Honey, no human could make that smell. It must be from one of the farms."

What?! This must be what OJ or Casey Anthony felt like, sheer disbelief in escaping a terrible crime. I just got away with murder—nostril murder.

Lesson learned: Everyone gets caught eventually, cheaters, liars, and casual farters. Out of guilt, I eventually told my wife who found the story *so* hilarious, that she told her Mom.

Have To Poop At the Coffee Shop But Can't Leave My Laptop

I've unintentionally stumbled into a Mexican standoff.

It's 1:07pm. Beautiful day outside. And I'm inside a coffee shop reeling in agony.

What happened?

I bought one of those giant $5 iced coffees, with absolutely no room for cream—as black as my soul. Over the course of the next hour I drained the beast like a slowly deflating tire. Then, in what was the calm before the storm, I had a window of 30 minutes of hyper activity. I was on YouTube, Facebook, Reddit, and then a little bit more YouTube.

After 25 minutes, I stopped the shenanigans and got down to brass tacks—writing. For those brief five minutes my fingers were fluttering over the keyboard, in an almost Lord of the Dance rhythmic bounce. Then my body shutdown.

An alarm started ringing on my colon like a nuclear reactor was melting down. Everyone is looking for the exit. I didn't have much time to make a decision. I couldn't leave my laptop in the coffee shop, since it would get stolen in a hummingbird's heartbeat. But if I brought the laptop into the bathroom, I'd be banned from the coffee shop and labeled a weirdo.

No matter the choice, I have lost.

I caved and put the laptop in my bag, which I regrettably brought into the bathroom. From here on out, you can do the math on what happened. I entered the bathroom after drinking a giant iced coffee. Your imagination should envision a calendar with the pages flying off, the leaves changing, snow melting, the birth of my children, them graduating from high school, and finally I walk out of the bathroom with gray hair and a cane.

I emerged unscathed to find my comfortable seat taken. Refusing to explain how caffeine runs through me like the Drain-o, I had to look for another seat.

In an act of horrible desperation I was forced to take a seat that wasn't next to a power charger, limiting my internet mooching to an hour at most.

This isn't the worst day of my life but it's in the top two.

Waiter Was Too Proud To Write Down Our Order And Forgot Half Of It

I'm raging, America.

There are few words, except maybe 321 or so to describe the emotions flowing through me. I've been accosted. Abused. Neglected. Tormented. Shamed.

Tonight, my waiter took us on a tour de turd because he was too proud to write down our order so he forgot about the premium chicken nuggets we ordered.

The restaurant is semi-nice. It's expensive, but not really worth the price except during happy hour. Our server was completely unprepared for someone as cheap as myself to show up at Happy Hour.

After browsing the Happy Menu and glossing over the $3 and $5 selections, our waiter approached with an empty holster. I knew this wouldn't end well. Very non-chalantly he asked, "What can I get for you guys?"

Still, with no notepad in sight, I go for the TKO. "Yes, we'll get the lemon garlic wings, edamame, mini burgers, ahi tuna sliders,…and chicken nuggets."

"Will that be all?" the server has the plumbs to say. I just rattled off the weekly grocery list for a family of four. No, actually, we also wanted the 72 ounce porterhouse. Come on, junior. It's not like I have a triple chin (only double).

The server spritzed over to the computer to punch in our order. 15 minutes later, a wave of glorious food landed on our table. Except our chicken nuggets were missing. Tragically, I didn't realize this until our server wandered off.

When he returned, I piped up "Are the chicken nuggets on the way?"

To which he responded, "You want an order of chicken nuggets? Sure." Oldest trick in the book—pretend like I never ordered the damn thing.

The kick in the pants was that by the time the chicken nuggets came, I wasn't hungry anymore. Should have never ordered them to begin with.

There was nothing happy about that hour. Bunch of amateurs.

The Butter Is Too Cold To Spread On My Banana Bread

Bless my Mom's heart, she sent me home with another loaf of her amazing banana bread. It's the kind that has little walnut bits and a sprinkling of brown sugar on top. That description doesn't do it justice, but it's incredible. If this was still the Wild West, where we didn't have a monetary system but traded goods, she'd be the richest person alive.

And I would still have problems.

Desperately in need of a snack, I went straight for the banana bread. Cut myself a few thick slices and took out the *I can't believe it's not butter**. But the stubborn butter was too cold to spread gracefully****. And you can't force butter to spread. If it's too cold to spread and you try anyway, you end up destroying the bread with the ferociousness of a chimp on antidepressants.

I am forced to put a slab of butter on the bread, heat it up in the microwave, but not for too long. Otherwise, the butter will melt and saturate just one spot of the bread instead of the entire canvas.

Just as alcohol can't freeze, we should be able to genetically engineer butter to not get beyond the density of being unspreadable. Do we know what scientists are working on? We hear a lot about them being in the lab, but if they aren't working on fixing this I can't imagine them doing anything productive.

No one has ever wanted just a hard brick of butter except demented kids in the "I'll eat anything" phase. It should always be spreadable. Get on it NASA.

Dear I Can't Believe It's Not Butter makers - It is 2012. We can believe it's not butter. Science has come pretty far. We can clone goats, go into space, print anything in 3D, some particles just went faster than the speed of light. You can change your name now. We'll take your word on it. Thanks. Respectfully yours, Ben.

**Was it my fault that the butter was unspreadable? Quite possibly. The butter was on the top shelf, right next to the freezer. Regardless, butter should always be spreadable.

Only Have $20s For The Vending Machine

I sound Daddy Warbucks ranting about this, but ask yourself: What year is it? OK, well then why is it impossible to buy anything from a vending machine without carrying around dollar bills and coins like a peasant?

I'm standing in front a vending machine at lunch time, unable to go outside and drive to a local deli because it's raining, and I don't want to get wet and smell like a dog. I'm mocked by the Jefferson(s) in my wallet. Like a gang of bullies teasing me, "Yeah, whatcha gonna do, tubs? Ain't buying no Twix with us."

Aha! I have change in my pocket. I pull out some coins and it adds up to 72 cents. I'm three damn cents short of sweet caramel serenity.

What is almost worse is the constant barrage of news articles saying that, "Oh, you'll just have to wave your phone in front of a vending machine and candy will shoot out like you hit the jackpot." No phone, no credit card, no dice.

Mints. All I can afford is mints.

I walked back to my desk with nothing but a roll of old man grandpa mints to nibble on the rest of the day. What an awful day, but at least my breath is temporarily good.

Snowed In So I Had To Pay Extra For Pizza Delivery

Another Saturday with a giant stain on it. There is absolutely perfect weather during the week. Then, when I have the weekend off Mother Nature takes a heaping deuce on my plans.

Tonight, I had dreams of going out into the world, picking up a pizza with the carry-out special coupon I received, and maybe getting a movie at the local Redbox. I know it's a lot to fit in for one night, but I wrote it in my mental planner and didn't want to miss the date.

But I'm stuck.

Outside, it's currently whiter than a Norwegian parade. Just snow everywhere. I can barely see my neighbor attempting to shovel my driveway for me (Minnesota nice). I guess the adage is true: "Man plans and God laughs." The big man must be rolling in the clouds, laughing about my night.

No discounted pizza for me. No Redbox. I'll be suffering through an old classic movie on Netflix that I haven't yet seen. Would have preferred something a little newer, but this will have to do for the evening.

Dostoevsky was right, "To live is to suffer."

Tried Exotic Food And Now Have Violent Diarrhea

I'm just a simple man from Minnesota. Male, middle class, and 100% Norwegian. Because of my boring complexion, I feel obligated to branch out and try adventurous food. Usually, that includes maybe a California roll, but today it was Thai food.

The choice of Thai food was not based on logic. The body of a Norwegian just isn't built for spicy food. It's built for consumption of stinky fish and maybe sour dough bread. Due to my love of horrible puns, I felt the need to repeatedly beat my wife over the head with the phrase, "Lets Thai something new for dinner!" until she reluctantly agreed on the condition I stop talking.

I've had Thai food before, though it was in a food court next to a Subway. This Thai restaurant was the real thing. Waiter barely spoke a lick of English, so I knew the food would be authentic and amazing.

When I ordered the Pad Thai, the server asked my spice preference. Having thought that my spice tolerance had been built up to a respectable level, due to my ability to handle spicy nacho cheese Doritos, I went with a 4 out of 5. This conveyed the message *"Hey, I've been around the block. This ain't my first Thai rodeo. Bring the heat."* The server gave a slight smirk and nodded.

When the food arrived, I could taste the heat before even taking a bite. This should have been the canary in the coal mine. With a large dose of chutzpah, I wolfed down the first bite.

Heat. That's all it tasted like. Heat.

My mouth lit up like a dry Christmas tree under hot lights. My upper lip and forehead began to sweat, while I did my best to show that I wasn't intimidated.

Bite two…

I'm a Kamikaze pilot on this suicide mission. My sweat glands are on full blast like sprinklers in a burning building. Of course this would be the time for server to come "check-in" and see how we are enjoying the food. The man looked at me like I was an abused puppy left at his doorstep.

I asked for the check and finished my food as fast as possible. Since the first bite, I knew that I had a ticking time bomb inside of me. The last thing I wanted was forced deployment in a public restroom.

With a 4 spice on a scale of 5, I was glued to the toilet, which felt like I was sitting on an erupting volcano. I can't fathom how food gets spicier than this. If I ordered a #5 spice, 20 minutes after digestion it would look like I was trying to smuggle a fire breathing dragon in my colon.

The drug commercials of the 90's warned what would happen if you took drugs. Apparently someone would go into your kitchen and destroy all of your eggs. But no one warned me of the consequences of spice for Norwegians.

The danger of spice should be passed down from generation to generation. I should be hearing stories from my Grandpa "You know Benjamin, your Great Uncle Sven died in the Korean War. He had mild-spiced noodles from a street vendor that tore apart his intestines. Learn from this."

Until Scandinavians can throttle our stupidity for trying bold spices, I don't see how we can evolve as a society.

Received Turkey Bacon Instead Of Real Bacon

Really don't know what type of society we are trying to form here. It's beyond question that our forefathers would not recognize America today. They would look upon America with the embarrassment of a father whose son just made the cheer squad. We might still call ourselves America, but this isn't America.

Today, at a trendy dumpster of a restaurant I ordered a bacon cheeseburger. Classic American lunch. When it arrived, I went after it like a python trying to swallow an alligator.

Woof.

With the recent rise in popularity of bacon, a certain group of sadists are determined to wreck the gluttonous experience of thy holy bacon. Apparently eating pigs is mean, but eating turkey floats their rowboat made from organic, biodegradable material.

Why make imitation bacon? Why? Bacon should be suing the manufacturers of Turkey Bacon for defamation, slander, libel, and treason.

This is just as bad as veggie burgers. It's not a burger. It's a veggie patty at best, but it's definitely not a burger.

Being given turkey bacon instead of delicious bacon is like finding out you took home a transvestite from the bar. You feel lied to, cheated, and want to erase the memory as quick as possible. This is how I felt taking a bite of Turkey Bacon. Oh, how far we have fallen?

Do your civic duty for America and call your lawmakers to restore the good name of bacon. Turkey bacon is for turkeys.

Asked For No Tomatoes On My Sandwich And Received a Surplus Of Tomatoes

After a long day at the office and a brief stint at the gym, I decided to reward myself with a sandwich from Jimmy Johns. Definitely not my first choice for a quick meal, but it was the most convenient.

So I ordered my sub, a #11 with NO tomatoes. The young chap takes my order and the assembly line of "sandwich artists" start piecing together the club sandwich at the speed of methamphetamine.

One assembly line worker says to maker of said sandwich "#11 with no tomatoes." Perfect...that is until I arrived at my apartment, sat down in front of the TV, cracked open a cold juice box, and found my sandwich had been vandalized.

Tomatoes...tomatoes...everywhere!

One by one I picked off God's unholy fruit. Along with the tomato ooze, my fingers were covered with excessive mayo. Maybe if Jimmy Jokes weren't so concerned with being "freaky fast" they could have thrown together a respectable piece of grub. This is a monstrosity. It's un-American. It's amateur.

Take a deep breath and put some pride in your sandwich creation.

I'll never eat there again! At least not until I'm moderately hungry and crunched for time. Then I'll probably eat there again.

Side note - Do we need to call people who make sandwiches artists? I've been in the trenches, making sub sandwiches and burning my arms on ovens. There is no artistry behind it. Mostly just people who wish they were doing something else. Any time you're adding an absurd noun to your title, you're a chump. Sandwich artist, social media samurai, marketing diva, _____ rockstar!, etc. Just do what you get paid to do and cut the glorified title. If everyone is an artist, no one is an artist.

Getting Pied In The Face

About once a year you hear of a polarizing figure, whether CEO or political commentator, getting a pie to the face from some hippy.

To someone in the Third World, this is something on a scale of "How did the universe originate?" type of incomprehensible. In America, not only do we have delicious pie, but we have enough to the point where we can weaponize it. Where impoverished counties might opt for rocks, whips, or shoes, we settle the hash with Lemon Meringue pie.

Getting a pie in the face may be humiliating, but at least it's a pie. Few times when people attempt to inflict you with harm, they do so with something so amazing. I wouldn't be that surprised if people said outrageous things so they could get more pie in the face. The nail that sticks up gets hammered down, the guy with crazy commentary gets delicious pie.

The crazier you talk, the more you get paid and the more likely it is that someone will throw a pie at your kisser. Where is the downside to being a nut bag? This is why so many wind bags are on cable news.

If you really hate this book and I mean *really* hate, not just indifferent, consider Apple pie with a caramel glaze. Actually, I take that back. I'll stick with Lemon Meringue, since Apple Pie would probably break my big nose.

Thanks in advance.

The Fancy Italian Restaurant Menu Didn't Have Pictures

I finally take the wife out for a fancy Italian meal, only to be embarrassed by a lackluster menu.

Sure there were dozens of fine sounding things, but not a single damn picture to whet my appetite. How am I supposed to know what's good if I don't have the visual connection? *How?* Especially when the menu is in Italian. Americans barely know English and most don't know the difference between "your" and "you're." How am I supposed to learn Italian?

I've become forever chained to the palatable Italian cuisine of The Olive Garden and their bountiful pictures. I don't even need to know the name. I can just order based on the pictures alone. This is great for me since I can't pronounce half of it anyway.

We have the technology. Now lets put a picture next to every item on every menu. It's what America wants, and more importantly, it's what America needs.

Does No One Care About Refilling The Peel And Eat Shrimp At The Chinese Buffet?

I'm on tilt right now.

It's completely out of character for me, but I'm ready to riot at the Chinese Buffet.

Every professional buffet enthusiast worth their weight in grease knows that on your first trip to the buffet, you just take a light sampling of every single item. On subsequent trips, you go back to the bread and butter of the buffet (obviously not literally since bread is a waste of stomach real estate). You find the absolute best items and bury your plate.

Three trips around the buffet and they still haven't refilled the peel and eat shrimp.

At what point do I start flipping tables and tossing chairs?

I've been patiently nibbling on the sesame chicken while hoping someone recognizes what is happening here.

Four trips and back. Nothing.

At this point in the meal I should be stuffed like a piñata while running circles around the buffet chanting, "U-S-A, U-S-A, U-S-A." Instead I'm holding a soft serve ice cream cone in my hand. It's pitiful.

All I want is peel and eat shrimp, a food that requires an enormous amount of effort to eat, but that's how tough I am. Instead of having a heaping pile of shrimp tales on my plate, I'm in the clean plate club. There's no carnage left behind to show how much I ate. Might as well have eaten a salad.

Your days are numbered, shrimps. Next time I'll be ready to occupy the buffet if I have to.

My Strawberry Milkshake Was Too Thick For My Straw Because They Used Real Strawberries

I write this with sore cheeks. It feels like I just tried to self-inflate a Macy's Day Parade balloon.

We have standards and consistencies to meet in most industries, yet the Milk Shake goes unregulated.

Prepare to write your Senator, America.

My strawberry milk shake was so thick, likely because the mom & pop shop insists on using real strawberries, that I couldn't use my straw. Like an idiot, I put the straw in and started sucking like a drowning man grasping for air. As I awkwardly attempted that first sip, my coworker inquired as to the quality of my shake. At this moment my straw was snagged on a strawberry. I quickly gave one of those "Eeesh..stuck…haha" looks and went back for another sip like I was trying to spear a fish.

On round two, a rain drop of milk shake hit my tongue. Glorious. I relayed the touch of heaven that embraced the tip of my tongue to my coworker and promptly proceeded to announce we needed napkins as I went to grab a spoon.

While I'm grateful the restaurant chose to use real strawberries, do blenders exist or do blenders exist? Maybe the problem is just that the straw is too small? After all, Panera Bread has straws built for today's American. They are about the circumference of a dime, as opposed to a pea, like most straws. The portions are getting bigger, but our ability to keep up is being governed by tiny straws.

It's time we evolve as a society. Imagine if they had giant milk shakes back in the days of *There Will Be Blood*. The famous line in the final scene would have been, "I drink your milkshake! And I'll drink it with a spoon because the straw gets clogged!"

Grow up, America.

Enough is enough! From this day forward I'm bringing my own straw when I order a milk shake.

Last Slice Of Heaven

I could give you an entire book of my food woes, but it would never end and you'd just get hungry.

Whenever I'd get close to finishing the book, my favorite pizza place would probably redraw their delivery zone to exclude me. And that would be one of the easier problems of the week. Lord knows what I'd do if the Taco Bell near my house was open anything less than 24 hours a day. That's how I sleep well at night. It's not just the sleep number bed and 600 thread count sheets. It's knowing that day or night, rain or shine, my Crunch Wrap Supreme thirst can be satiated.

There are too many other problems in the First World and most of them start with being First World Poor.

FIRST WORLD POOR

I'm The Poorest Person I Know

Poverty in America is real. These stories recall in graphic detail, some of the trials and tribulations of the common man.

I don't have a 27" iMac. I only have the 21".

I was only able to lease a new car instead of buy it.

I have to get the cheapest organic cheese at Whole Foods.

I can only afford White Chocolate Mochas four days a week.

I can only afford the deluxe car wash, not the premium deluxe.

Only single stuff Oreos are in my budget.

I'm unable to buy fair trade coffee and must consume coffee that was unfairly traded.

It's not easy being me. Life dealt a rough hand. Grab the tissues now, because you're about to hear horrible sob stories about being First World Poor.

I Have To Hand Wash My Dishes Before Putting Them In The Dishwasher

I really don't understand why we have dishwashers. What's the point of a dishwasher if I have to hand wash the dishes before putting them in?

It's like the dishwasher is chugging along, making "Whoosh" sounds and then says, "Meh, that's good enough. What's on Netflix?" and just gives up. We can send a man to the moon, but can't get a dishwasher to get all the pizza sauce off my plate. What gives, America?

I have to slave away over a pile of dirty dishes that I can't make clean by the dishwasher alone. "Dishwasher" is far too generous a name since it implies actual washing happening. "Dish splash some hot water like a baby in the bathtub and hope for the best" is a more apt name.

This doesn't happen with any other products. I don't have to stick my bread in the oven before putting it in the toaster. I don't hand wash my clothes before putting them in the washing machine.

In an age when robots are supposedly taking everyone's jobs, they can't take one of the very few that I actually do at home. And it's maddening.

My Dryer Didn't Completely Dry My Jeans So I Had To Spend Another 75 cents

Damn damp dryer. The apartment I'm living in currently runs a dryer monopoly. There is *no* competition, *no* pressure to excel, and *no* functional dryer. Just jeans that after the cycle has completed, it feels like they just took a walk through the car wash.

This problem isn't isolated to this apartment alone. It has happened at every apartment I've lived at, which might be why I rarely wash my pants. This isn't to stay I'm walking in filth. I Febreeze. I just prefer my pants dry.

This morning I did a quick load of laundry before work because I had nothing to wear. The dryer finished just as I was about to sprint out the door. I pulled out my jeans to find them moderately damp. Now I have absolutely no choice but to walk around until lunch feeling like I peed my pants. If anyone so much as grazes against my knee I fumble to explain "Oh, I didn't pee my pants. Bad dryer. You know how that goes, right?...Right? Is this thing on?"

How am I supposed to do anything productive when every effort is for naught? It's a lot to expect a dryer to *dry* something, I'm aware. But my modest expectations shouldn't make me feel like I soiled my pants.

Getting Paid To Save Lives Is Boring

I'm not a hero. Let's clear the air before there is any confusion. It just happens that I donate my precious plasma in exchange for money. Technically, it could be called "selling" plasma, but I think donating has a better ring due to the charitable connotations.

It's really the only way to make decent money as a young employable middle class white man. I give them an hour of my time and they give me $25-40. But man, is it boring.

For that hour I'm pretty much left alone with my thoughts. Unless of course, a homeless man next to me is babbling on about space ships and rhinos. Then I'm falling into my Minnesota nice accent of "Uh huh, Yeah. Ohhh sure." It's as gross as it sounds in your head.

The least the plasma clinic could do is throw up a few TVs with Keeping up with the Kardashians or The Bachelor. We're saving lives here. A little entertainment wouldn't kill them.

Right now my mind has wandered from where I left my toenail clippers to wondering what that rusty smell is. This isn't a humane work environment, especially for a hero, like myself.

If this is how we treat our heroes, how do we treat the common man? Priorities America, priorities.

Someone Didn't Refill The Brita

After long day of lying on the couch eating some of the saltiest chips known to mankind, through shear tyranny of will I found the strength to get off the couch and get some water.

When I opened the door, I dropped my plastic cup in slow motion. The Brita was empty. Some sadist drained it and put it back as a cruel joke.

Like a stranded tourist finally discovering a river of clean water on the mountain, I lapped up the tap water out of pure desperation—on par with a dog drinking from the garden hose.

Head under and slurping it up. It tasted raw, irony (as in iron-ish, not ironic), and full of contaminants. It's no way for a man to live. But bordering on dehydration, I had no choice.

The economy is bad, but this is one of those stories you don't hear on the news. Likely too graphic in detail to enable the average American to sleep peacefully. Yet, it's reality for me.

Just try to sleep comfortably tonight knowing that I had to drink water straight from the tap. It's impossible.

Cut My Own Hair And It's a Nightmare

I had a delightful weekend. Went to a movie, ate at my favorite restaurant, and got to catch up on some sleep.

I'm not sure what type of weekend my hair had. On Sunday night, fresh off the purchase of a set of hair clippers, I gave myself a haircut, took a shower, and called it a night.

The next morning I woke up, looked in the mirror and wondered when my hair went to Lilith Fair over the weekend. Cutting your own hair is a horrible decision.

I wouldn't have to go through the pain of cutting my own hair if getting it cut by a professional wasn't so awkward.

It starts out bad - *"How do you want your hair cut?"* Ummm…just shorter? I don't know what to say. And it's not like I can say "Make me look like Dolph Lundgren," without them thinking I'm super weird.

Once we decide on them making my hair shorter, we then get to slide head-first into awkward conversation. It's almost like I'm on a job interview, but I have to pay at the end of it.

"What do you do for work? Where do you live?" It's hard to be interesting when I'm not even interested in myself.

Then the barber will hold up the tiny mirror and ask how the back of my hair looks. I have no idea what to say other than good. If I say I don't like it, what are they going to do? "Alright, let me rub in some growth cream so I can re-cut your hair." Can't unscramble an egg.

So I continue to cut my own hair and look like a goon.

Apartment Dishwasher Is Too Loud

Why has nothing has been done to combat obscenely loud dishwashers? In our tiny apartment whenever I try to watch something on TV, every two seconds I hear, "Whooosh…Whooosh" It's endless, until it ends in 30 minutes.

My reward for interrupting the running marathon of *The Wire* to clean dishes is the roar of the dish washing beast, which made it impossible to enjoy watching TV.

The only solution is to wash the dishes by hand, but that would be ridiculous. Then I couldn't enjoy the LED TV I just bought and I might as well be living in a cave, hunting and gathering my own food too.

How have dishwashers not advanced with quieter technology? Or maybe they have and I've been too poor my whole life to know any better. There is currently no reason why most new cars should be quieter than dishwashers. A metal box that travels 70mph and runs on gasoline is quieter than most dishwashers.

The only solution I see is paper plates. Not classy. Probably terrible for the environment, but what option do I have? Not watch TV for 30 minutes? The dishwasher would still be so loud I couldn't think.

I have no choice. Sorry, Al Gore.

Neighbor Stopped Paying For Internet I'm Mooching

Day 3 of living in a cold, dark, barren world with no connection to the World Wide Web. I have no idea what made the front page of Reddit, what those funny cats are up to, and can barely remember the lunch I tweeted about yesterday.

When looking for a place to live, I made sure there was an open internet connection. Now three months in, I can receive the signal, but the internet isn't working. It's such a simple fix too. Just unplug the router, wait 10 seconds and plug it back in. It's that simple. But they're probably old and can't get a hold of their kids in college to tell them what to do. So I'm stuck with no internet and the only solution I have is to go to the local coffee shop, buy the cheapest thing possible, and then spend 4 hours getting my internet fuel. And during all of that, pray that I don't have to make a bowel movement or else the whole trip will be ruined.

I'm not sure what to do. Because the second I get a connection of my own, the neighbors will fix the connection making me feel like a damn fool.

So I hopelessly wait. Carry on, internets. Keep LOL'ing without me.

Play me off, keyboard cat.

I Don't Have an A/V Input In My Car So I Have To Listen To My iPhone with Headphones

Ah, yet another embarrassing ride home from work. You'd think my chariot that is known to most people as a hail-dented 1998 Chevy Lumina that originally came with a tape deck because my Dad had more tapes than CD's in 1998, which then required me to foot the bill for the glorified 1 disc CD deck, would be a delight to ride in, but it's a mess (Run on sentence is done. Take a deep breath.).

Because of the limited range of a Compact Disc, I'm forced to listen to my new iPhone whenever I'm in the car. The white ear buds are my scarlet letter. A sign of my thrift.

Plus, with the air conditioning out, I have to drive with the windows cracked. Couple that with my affinity to sing along with *Les Miserables* at the top of my pipes (I do an incredible Jean Valjean), putting on a free show for the surrounding cars.

Papa Government gave everyone a rebate to switch to DTV, how about an A/V input for every car? I'm just spit-balling ideas here. It's at least as important as helping struggling homeowners.

Until then, I'll continue to be "that guy" driving in my Chevy Lumina with iPod headphones, singing the hits.

Paid In Cash And Now I Have To Carry Around Coins

This is annoying. In one of the rare instances that I paid in cash (technically I was forced to since I didn't spend over $5), I received 94 cents in change. As I slipped the handful of change into my pocket, I felt the sudden urge to tighten my belt another notch.

What a curse change is. It's no wonder the Saca…saca…whatever her name is didn't catch on (My Grandpa pronounces them Sa-ca-ca-wee-yah's, but I have no clue if that's right).

Yes, please let me pay with giant dollar coins that aren't made of chocolate. What a tease. Like that was ever going to work in America. Ironically, it costs more than $1 to buy a chocolate coin than a dollar coin. You'd think it would at least be an even trade.

Coins are the poopstain of the monetary system. All you need to know about spare change is that two types of people love it; the homeless and old men.

Homeless only love it because it's money. They'd take dollar bills or payments via Paypal seven days a week and twice on Wednesday if they could. But old men love change because they enjoy jingling it around in their pocket with the tenacity of a Salvation Army Bell Ringer.

Can we abolish change?

Few things frustrated me more than Obama's 2008 Presidential slogan "Change we can believe in." Not because he wanted to change policies, but because he talked about change favorably. Enough positive associations with change and people will view all change as positive, from policies to old men rattling coins in their pocket.

It's time for a change from change.

The 2 Setting On My Car's Air Conditioning Is Too Timid While 3 Is Too Cold

If you've learned anything about life so far, it's that you should obsess over the horrible minute details like I do. My car is another perpetrator driving up my blood pressure.

In the dog days of Summer, air conditioning is a constitutional right. But my car can't handle that responsibility.

When I put the air conditioning on the 2 setting I'll hear whoever is on the passenger seat say "Turn the air on, it's 95 degrees out." It's supposedly on, but I can't feel the effect of it.

So then I bump up the setting to #3, which if we lived in a rational world would be a proportional upgrade from the power of #2. Instead we go from light Spring breeze to hovercraft power.

It takes about 2 seconds for my car to sound like a jet engine about to explode.

Besides the noise, it just becomes way too cold too quickly. That's no way to live, from hot to cold to freezing.

Where is the government regulation on proportional fans? And if someone does do something about the fans, how about making car horns a little bit more interesting?

Pointless Car Alarm Woke Me Up From a Nap

While 10 minutes into a deep blissful afternoon nap set to the soundtrack of golf, a car alarm went off outside my apartment, snapping me back to reality. It obviously wasn't my car since it doesn't have an alarm, but my nap chi was thrown out of whack.

Let's examine the paragraph above. In no point did my locomotion of thought say, *"MY GOD! A car alarm! Someone's car is being stolen! Someone call 911!"*

The car alarm has passed the point of ever being useful again.

With how advanced technology has come, shouldn't car alarms be able to distinguish between a portly lady bumping her rump against the mirror while getting out of her car and grand theft auto?

I'm surprised people still break into cars. I remember when I used to be afraid of leaving my CD case visible in the car for fear that someone would break into my car solely for my CD collection. They probably would have been slightly disappointed by ABBA's Gold Collection, but it would have been devastating for me. Now they cut out the middle man and just steal from labels.

Society shouldn't allow people to have car alarms in any average car. Save them for the BMWs, Maseratis, or Bentleys, not the mom fumbling with groceries in one hand and mashing buttons on the keychain in the other.

Enough. It's all noise pollution.

While we are at it, we need new car horns. The standard car horn rarely has any effect. This might get annoying, but if we don't try it, we'll never know…

I'd like to see these car horns:
- The Road Runner's "Meep, Meep"
- The sound of a giant sigh.

- Kevin Spacey via Superman Returns yelling "WRONG!" Look it up on YouTube and leave a comment like everyone does "First World Problems book sent me here."
- The Jeopardy Theme
- (Read by Oprah) It's Grrr-reeeeeaaaan!

The Battery In My Key Fob Died

The latest social stamp of my poorness is that the key fob on my car no longer works.

You know the scene in scary movies when a stumbling ditz is running to her car in high heels, and when she finally gets to the car she fumbles with her keychain for 30 seconds, eventually getting herself slaughtered? You know that scene? Anyway, that's me right now. I'm the dummy.

There are so many benefits to having a key fob, once they're revoked I'm like a raccoon on the side of the road, just waiting to get hit by traffic. What if the next time I'm walking to my car in a deserted parking ramp at 3am, someone tries to rape me? Weirder things have happened. I'd be done for.

What about when I forget where I parked? It's guaranteed to happen every time I visit the Mall of America. I walk out with two hands full of shopping bags and have no idea where to go. With the key fob, I could hit the lock button and hear a toot off in the distance.

There is nothing I can do, but get a new car now. I refuse to be the guy who gets mocked behind the scenes at the dealership. It's obvious the 1998 hail-dented Chevy Lumina isn't key fob worthy. It's a luxury through and through, but it's not so easy to have your cake taken away from you.

Until I can afford a new car, I'll be leaving myself open to being the number 1 target for sexual predators in dimly lit parking ramps between the hours of 3am-5am.

Wish me luck, guys.

Woke Up Freezing In The Middle Of The Night But Was Too Tired To Turn Off The Fan

I'm on E right now. My tank is empty, but I'm writing out of the goodness of my heart and the hope that I may get a chuckle out of someone. Last night I got maybe 4 hours of sleep. That's even a bad night of sleep for someone who has insomnia and a crying new born. I have neither.

I awoke around 1am after retiring to bed at exactly 10:36pm CST. About a minute after my head hit the hypoallergenic pillow, I was sawing logs.

Then came the first awakening.

Around 1am I awoke shivering like a starved meth addict. It's the middle of Summer and my face felt like an icicle. The covers hadn't fallen off and I didn't sleepwalk and crawl into the freezer. Since laying down to bed, the temperature outside dropped like the desert, rendering my fan unnecessary.

But it was still on full-blast right on my face, not even oscillating!

This is where the rational person says, "So turn it off, dummy." Classic Monday morning quarterbacking. I'm still super tired. I can barely open my eyes. It's just not that easy to get up, walk three feet and turn it off.

Secondly, I did some quick math and if I shut off the fan, there is a 65% chance I'll wake up sweating (and sweaty). I don't like those odds.

With an inhuman amount of will, I went back to bed. For the next four hours I bounced in and out of sleep, dreaming about ice skating naked. Weird things happen when you're cold and delirious.

All this huffing and puffing lead to a solution. I need to get The Clapper hooked up to the fan, making it possible for me to turn off the fan with a single clap. I just hope I don't start applauding in my sleep now.

There Are Glasses Full of Water All Over My House

I hit the breaking point tonight. While watching *The Bachelor* (Don't judge), I noticed just how messy and dirty my house had become. Looking around it was easy to notice one consistent theme.

Water glasses. Everywhere.

I blame my wife for 87% of the glasses since She likes to fill a glass, take two sips and quietly forget about the glass. She isn't totally to blame though. Once a year I'll accidentally leave a water glass sitting out while I'm doing hundreds of push-ups and forget about it.

It becomes a massive problem. My living room looks like the end of the movie Signs, glasses half-full (optimist) of water everywhere. I don't know what to do with all of them. Sometimes I'll take a sip out of one if I'm too lazy or involved in a show to get off the couch. You'd think water doesn't expire, but some of it tastes like a stale sock.

What I need is one of those 64 ounce plastic mugs from a gas station. But then what do I do if those start getting left everywhere?

There is no winning. Water all over the place and no motivation to move it.

At least if my house catches fire, it might put itself out.

Because Poverty Is Relative, I'll Always Be Poor

Looking back through history, it's likely that I'll always be poor.

The problem with poverty is that it's relative. The poor person today has a better life than a King did 200 years ago. As a society, if we could pick just one definition of being poor and stick to it, there is a small chance I could escape that label.

Poor today in the First World is simply being 10 years late to having something.

Things the rich had 10 years before poor people:
- Color TV
- Cable TV
- Air conditioning
- Cars
- Computers
- Cell phones

Eventually everything trickles down, but the waiting is awful. Brookstone is only a futuristic store for poor people. The rich can take whatever they like. The poor get added to society's waiting list.

Though I'm forever on the slow-incline of First World Poor, there is always shopping. If we Americans are good at anything, it's shopping. Even if we don't have money, we are extremely good at shopping.

Not sure if being poor makes the shopping experience worse, but it's not good.

SHOPPING

Shopping Is Miserable In The First World

If anyone knows how difficult shopping can be, it's citizens of the First World.

You can't buy much in the third world and everything that you do buy is generally within a two-mile radius of where you live. If a street vendor doesn't have what you want, tough. In the First World, you're forced to drive to every location until you find it. We don't even get the luxury of bartering.

What follows is the account of a man who carries many scars from shopping. I've been in the Armani-coated trenches. I know what it's like to return gifts the day after Christmas because you're anxious to get what you really want. I know what it's like to bravely venture inside Costco on the weekend, if only for the food samples. I've had to navigate unlawful parking lots, wait for someone to write a check, and dealt with awkward cashiers.

This is my salutation to struggling shoppers. Keep shopping till you drop from sheer exhaustion or bad Chinese food at the sketchy food court.

The only thing that's always in stock is my First World Shopping Problems.

I Always Pick The Wrong Line To Stand In

Sometimes I swear I'm in *The Truman Show*. If I have two lines to choose from, there is a 90% chance I will pick the wrong line. Once I make the decision for a line, about 20 seconds later someone will get in line behind me and by that point I'm stuck. There is no going back.

A few people in front of me pay with cash. No big deal. I don't care that they need change or that the cashier has to crack a new roll of nickels. Meh. Just means more time to play *Words With Friends* on my phone.

Hmmm. The other line is moving quite swimmingly. People mostly paying with credit cards.

Checks, huh? You're really going to pay with a check? What year is it? Right. Are you writing your grandson a birthday present, grandma? It was denied. Oh, you're going to write a second one? Why would you question the authenticity of a coupon? It's 35 damn cents. You need sense, not cents. Am I losing my mind?

Who makes conversation with the cashier at the expense of holding up the line behind you? The cashier doesn't care that you're remodeling your kitchen. Let me buy my one family-sized bag of Cheetos and be gone from here.

Each transaction takes a year off my lifespan. It's the appreciation I get for supporting big box retailers when I could just buy everything online. There is no wrong line online. With the internet you're never in line—you're online. Does your head hurt yet?

The solution to all of this is self checkout lanes.

I take that back. Self checkout lanes are the worst thing ever invented...

Self Checkout Lanes Are Ruining America

In 1992, Dr. Howard Schneider birthed a system that would come to frustrate and ruin a quick run to the grocery store: The self checkout lane.

Self checkout lanes are a lot like communism. Sounds like Heaven on paper, but quickly becomes Hell once implemented. The supermarket has become the modern day gulag. They are ruining America.

The Idea:
I love the idea of a self checkout lane. When I'm in a hurry and buying a single desperation item like a plunger or extra thick bacon, I can quickly do my business without the questioning gaze of the judging cashier. In a world full of adults with common sense, it's a great system where we don't have to answer to "the man" whether we want paper or plastic.

Reality:
The reality is dark and cold.

The typical scenario looks like this:
Of the four or five self checkout registers, only one person will know what they're doing.

A hipster kid in their 20's with earbuds in, rings up his frozen pizza and is gone before anyone else has moved. The rest of the group will be composed of a do-it-herself Mom with 40 items, an elderly gentleman not quite sure about this technology, and a confused woman whose scanned item isn't registering. She is unsure if she should seek help or keep mashing buttons that don't work.

To quote Peter Parker, "With great power comes great responsibility." We've given all the wrong people at the supermarket power and they're responsible for my unhappiness.

Here are the people and problems who wreck self checkout lines:

Unexpected item in the check-out area
This has happened to me at least three times. Suddenly, the screen tells me there is an unexpected item in the check-out area. I have no idea what it's trying to infer. It's certainly not unexpected that I'm buying ice cream.

Old People Confused by Technology
Some of the older folk make selections on the screen with the delicacy of a professional chess player. It's not that hard to realize "Credit card" means you have to pay with a credit card.

People Buying Fruit
"Ahhhhhh, no UPC label to scan!!!" Not that difficult to find Banana while searching alphabetically. If you struggle with that, what can you do? Do you add any value to society?

Person With a Ridiculous Amount of Items
The people who do this are the same people who bring 20 items to the 10 items or less lane. Just going about their day, ho-hum, without realizing or caring that half of their local community is waiting for them.

People Who Buy Alcohol or Cough Medicine
Obviously you're going to need assistance from a cashier anyway, so why even step in the self checkout lane? Why? If it's your first time buying cough medicine, that's understandable, but come on! Keep up with society.

I'm afraid America just isn't ready for self checkout. It needs to go into beta, where only a select group can use the machines while apprenticing in some of society's laggards.

Until then, I'll be standing in the wrong line waiting for a cashier to ring me up.

Can't Tell If The Person In Front Of Me Is Standing In Line Or Not

When I was around the age of 13, aliens came down and probed me with a magnet that attracts awkward situations. I'm 95% confident that happened.

Today, I had the pleasure of one of those "Are you in line or just reading the menu?" moments at McDonald's for no good reason.

First of all, if you're just reading the menu, make sure you are as far back as possible. None of this orbiting around other people in line is called for. In or out. Pick a side.

Also, there is no reason to read the menu at McDonald's. The menu almost never changes besides the McRib coming and going like a negligent father. Who really needs to take their time to formulate an order?

This is where those line-guides they have at the bank are helpful. There's no guessing about who is in line. You're either in the queue or not. Though there is the issue of the person in the front of the line not hearing the tiny teller squeaking, "I can help whoever is next!" Then the person behind them has to direct them to the teller. The bank line has faults, but it's an improvement upon the unregulated jungle of fast food.

In this case, I rolled the dice and just went straight to the back of the line, cutting off the drifter. If he was in line, there's a chance he would have said something, but most people are too passive, especially in Minnesota, to say anything.

Were they in line? I have no idea. But I am now.

Ate Too Much Food And I Don't Have a Plunger

The toilet just overflowed like a slot machine hitting 7-7-7. There goes my favorite pair of socks.

My roommate and I don't own a plunger. I'm not sure if that's due to the both of us being used to industrial power flow toilets or the increasing feminization of society, but a plunger we are without.

The only logical option is to pay a visit to the convenience store right next to my apartment. It's a little Greek place that sells Gyros*, funyons, and frozen pizzas.

As I walked in the store, I spotted the overpriced plunger almost immediately. Fantastic. But I can't bring it straight to the counter. The guy will think I'm a freak who clogged my toilet and rushed down here in a sweaty mess. I made the brilliant decision to somewhat mask my purchase by buying at least one additional item. I grabbed something I was already going to buy; an energy drink.

I approached the counter with the swagger of a modern man just going about his normal day. Then the absurdity of the situation set in.

Here I am, a man dressed rather sheepishly in basketball shorts and a white t-shirt with either a paint or mustard stain on it. On the counter I've laid down a plunger and an energy drink.

Thinking the energy drink would mask the plunger was the dumbest thing I've ever done. Energy drinks don't mask, they amplify whatever else you're buying. Buying a book and energy drink? You're about to read like a boss. Buying an energy drink and protein bar? You're about to max out on the bench press. Buying an energy drink and plunger? You flushed a chocolate redwood down the toilet that the human condition alone isn't prepared to handle.

The clerk must be thinking, "Here is a guy without much going on. Clearly isn't dressed to societal standards. Has a terrible diet that caused him to lodge a stool the size of New Jersey in the toilet and buy a plunger. And it's a big enough mess that he has to buy an energy drink, lest he wear himself out huffing and pumping away."

I left the convenience store embarrassed, but on a mission. Should I be proud or ashamed that this wasn't a one-use purchase, but a reusable resource? I'm fiscally proud, but emotionally shamed.

America needs to make up its damn mind. Do you pronounce it Gyro or Euro?

Returning Items On The Day After Christmas Is a Horrible Idea

What a terrible hangover to start the day.

Not a booze hangover - the Christmas hangover.

Holidays are supposed to be a time of merriment, jubilation, and excessive eating, but they end up just being exhausting. Today I spent three hours returning gifts so I could buy the items I really wanted.

Bless all the kind people who gave me various gifts, but they missed the mark, if ever so slightly.

Why didn't I wait a few days before returning the gifts? Why don't you wait a few days before your next meal? Not so easy, is it? When I get a present, I have the patience of a mosquito at a nude beach. I want to use the present or return it for something better. Simple as that.

So I wait for the lady in front of me to return a George Foreman grill. She must have received two of them because no sane person would ever return the gift that keeps on giving. I could write an entire book about cooking perfect sausage links on that grill.

After three hours of waiting, I'm finally free to exchange Season 6 of *LOST* for *Saved by the Bell* - Seasons 3 & 4. Such a good trade. If I had the time, I'd flip houses and make millions, but I'll be too busy watching Zack Morris talk on his giant cell phone and AC Slater wearing tank tops like he stole 'em.

Until next year, day after Christmas returning chumps.

Target Has Too Many Handicap Spots

On this lovely afternoon, I found myself driving down to the local Target for a few miscellaneous items. I had no idea I would be greeted with such wasted potential. What I saw is a parking lot at capacity with 12 parking spaces completely empty. 12 empty handicap spaces. Nothing, but an abandoned shopping cart to fill the empty void.

Do we really need that many handicap spots? I had to park two football fields away from Target, just in case a jury of handicapped people showed up at the same time. I expect more from you Target. And I also expect more from our society.

Will no one speak out against the superfluous handicap parking spaces? Target isn't the only store guilty. Look at any major retailer. They all have blue and white paint on their hands.

I sound like a terrible person ranting about this, but at a certain point it becomes ridiculous. What if the parking lot was 50% handicap spots? 80%? Then what? To some people you can never have enough handicap spots and you can never spend enough on education, despite kids today being dumb as rocks.

Fear not, America. I have a solution.

Parking spots should be arranged by BMI. Those with BMI's off the chart near the pre-Subway Jared level, should be forced to park at the back of the parking lot. At the other end of the scale you have Lance Armstrong parking right next to the entrance. Can't deny that the man has earned it.

We're one step parking space closer to solving all of America's problems.

Cashier Awkwardly Gave Back My Change

I've never met someone who had stronger feelings regarding how cashiers hand back change than me. It has been driving me up a wall with vaulted ceilings and today I hit the bricks.

While getting a strawberry / banana smoothie (smoothie for a smooth guy) I paid with a $10 bill, leaving my change to $4.43. The cashier, a friendly young girl, handed me back the change all at once, coins on top of bills, like some sloppy open-faced monetary sandwich. As she attempted to drop the change into my hand, a dime went straight into my smoothie and sunk like a chunk of coal.

After a brief "You spilled the milk" pause, I said, "It's not a big deal." She retorted with a disgusted face, "But it's a dime. Gross." Out of courtesy to the cashier, for who all I know, has to pay for each wasted smoothie, I offered to drink the smoothie with a dime in it. Not ideal, but I'm nice. She looked at me like I just asked to dig through the trash for banana peels.

"I'll make you another," she said while tossing my smoothie into the trash. She didn't learn a lesson. How many more people will she give back change to poorly? It's like a guy totaling his car while drunk and you give him another car. He's still going to get drunk and mow down joggers on the sidewalk. I totally would have drank that smoothie, too. Who cares if I swallow a dime?

How to hand back change:

In this example, the change we are handing back is $4.89. Simply hand back the coins first, then give back the one dollar bills. Always lead with coins. There is no reason to lump them all together. They don't mix. One or the other first. Unless you like being awkward, then give back both at once and apologize when the change hits the counter for the billionth time.

Black Friday Is For The Birds

I had my most productive Black Friday yet! I woke up 20 minutes ago and saved $160 on Amazon. I have beef, serious beef with Black Friday.

Whenever I see the line of people waiting for some major retailer, I want to walk up to them, grab them by the shoulders and whisper, "Hey, there is something called the internet. You can get even better deals there." But if I did that, I'd deprive their life of meaning for a week.

I can understand the people who show up around 3am. It's kinda fun, there's the camaraderie of standing outside together striving toward the common goal of being a cheap bastard. But the people who line up *days* (yes, plural) in advance, America has no need for them.

If you can afford to spend 3 days, be them vacation days or not, to wait in line at Best Buy to save $30 bucks on a Blu Ray player, you've got nothing to offer society. Pack it up. Fold up shop. Turn off. You're done. We can make it the rest of the way without you.

By lining up for days outside of big box retailers, you're essentially telling everyone that you don't value your time. If your time was worth $1 an hour, you wouldn't be there. You'd be making money by providing a service society values.

I could profit off all the people waiting in line. Go around selling lottery tickets and chewing tobacco. I'd get filthy rich. Partly because those people haven't showered in days and I would make a disgusting amount of money from them. But I won't go through with it. That's how much I hate people lining up for Black Friday.

It's called the internet. Look into it.

The Person In Front Of Me Had 22 Items In The 10 Items Or Less Line

I'm not one to do the "slippery slope" thing of "But if we give women the right to vote, all men will be voted out of office, and everyone will get cooties and die." With that said, letting someone with 22 items in the 10 items or less line will eventually lead to riots, an overthrow of government, and the end of society as we know it.

The cashier who permitted the worst person in the world to take upward of 22 items into the 10 items MAX line is nudging our society into a soft chaos. Granted, she did make a whimpering comment about it.

"This is *a little* more than 10 times."

"Haha. Yeah, I guess it is."

Then silence. This happened in California, so it's not really a shock that their economy is so awful. Because there is no way this would fly in somewhere like Texas. In Texas, they'd castrate you for even drifting your cart close to the 10 item aisle. Not in California. "Wheeeeeeeeee! Wheeeeeeeeee! Wahoooo!" I imaging the old frump in front of me singing to herself and she tears down society's mores.

It's a slippery slope. Today we let people with 22 items into the 10 items or less line, tomorrow the national language is German and we're all wearing Lederhosen.

Is that what you want, America?

It's Impossible To Buy Just One Thing At Costco

What's there to hate about Costco? They offer cheap gas, cheap groceries, and cheap hot dogs? What isn't so American about that?

I hate the fact that I can't go to Costco for a single item. I live a stone's throw from a Costco, but find myself making the longer drive to Cub Foods for the single items. It's just too intense.

I've received enough of the cockeyed glances at the register when picking up a hot tub sized bucket of ice cream or enough TP to stock an Old Country Buffet for a month. It's impossible to buy a single item from Costco without looking like a freak with a mini frozen taco fetish.

Something needs to be done for the people who only want a single item. Why not have a one item or less line? Let people self-checkout, or maybe not, but give them a designated space. By giving them a specific aisle, you can let them be assured that making a special trip just for a box of 100 taquitos is completely normal.

Until that day, I'll just be silently suffering the embarrassment of a crazy shopper while in line. At least I'll be providing some stories for the cashier to tell around the dinner table, *"So this one guy came in and all he bought was a 12 pack of deodorant. Smell much? Right? Am I right, guys?"*

Thanks for the embarrassment.

Costco Is Full of Sample Hoarders

Today was my first time experiencing bulk in totem. Sure, I've been on the occasional trip to Sam's Club with my Mom as a kid, but this is my first full out dive into the depravity of middle class America.

Saturday and Sunday afternoons are a terrible time to visit Costco, yet mass crowds continue to schlep themselves to the warehouse, navigate the overcrowded parking lot, and flash a plastic card at the AARP member feigning attention.

This Sunday afternoon was a cluster.

I try to think well of people. I like to think people are generally good and mean well. Unfortunately, it's just not true. Anyone who says that hasn't been to Costco on the weekends, where ordinary people turn into vultures, hovering over an 80 year old woman in a hair net prepping a tray full of chicken nuggets.

It becomes nearly impossible to sample anything at Costco without looking like a starving zombie.

Four kinds of people who sample food at Costco:

The Camper: What shame? The Camper isn't here to deal with any funny business. They want their sample and they are willing to wait for it to pop out of the microwave, however long that may be.

The Fart in the Wind: Appears out of nowhere to snatch the last sample. Here and gone, like a fart in the wind.

The Double Down: The man (almost always a man) who grabs two samples as the stock dwindles. Yeah, one is for the "wife"…right.

The Boomerang: Got snuffed on their last effort, yet can't let go the thought of getting a cheese pizza sample. Because who has any idea what frozen cheese pizza tastes like? They'll continue on the tour-de-samples until they try everything twice.

The Pro (ahem...me): It would be a lie to say that I'm not one of the best samplers in the country. I'll go toe-to-toe, nay, salmon spread triscuit-to-salmon spread triscuit with anyone. When sampling I'll project that I'm interested, but not desperate. I don't lurk. I casually push my cart at a slight stroll until I see tray being lifted over the iron curtain and pounce with the grace of a gazelle. *"Oh, you have a sample going on? I didn't notice. Well, this looks like something I may buy. May I dare show my taste buds the joy of chicken pot pie? Wonderful!"*

In business it is often said that you should take someone golfing or to a restaurant and watch how they treat the wait staff if you want to see their true colors. A modern form of this personality polygraph should be shopping at Costco on a Sunday afternoon.

Patrons act with the same tenacity as if the old sample lady is putting out a tray of Dixie cups filled from the fountain of youth. Everyone forgets that they're getting a bird bite of a cheap Chimichanga.

In the land of the wealthy & obese we freak out over free samples. In this case, it's generally the youth who are the victims. It's the AARP card carriers and the soccer moms who have the samples in a death grip. They aren't shy about it either. They watch the sample prepper behind the steel microwave put together a tray of crackers, which they flock to like pigeons, sometimes grabbing two. It's depressing.

I'm afraid there is no solution. Except to maybe spike the samples with Norplant. Not much Norplant, but enough to guarantee that if someone has more than 3 samples they'll be rendered unable to have children. I don't want anyone who is obsessed with chicken nugget samples to be reproducing and I doubt you do either.

My ideas coupled with a little bit of help from you, and we are on our way to making a great society.

Hair Nets Are Distracting

I kind of love The Costco Grill.

Do I have a problem with it? Not really, since it's more of a lingering fascination.

There is a 20-something guy who works the cash register / pizza oven 90% of the time I'm at Costco. He has a goatee and because Costco makes you wear hair nets, he has to wear a beard net for his goatee.

Now every time I get a hot dog I think, "This guy really loves his goatee. He loves it enough to put up with a ridiculous looking beard net, as if goatee hair really sheds. He's committed to that goatee. No way would I keep a petty goatee if I had to wear a net. Imagine if he applied that dedication to other areas of his life. Might be a Senator or manager of a Papa John's franchise. Who knows?!"

The hot dog purchase gets awkward as I just stand there pontificating to myself on his goatee, far past when the transaction has ended.

Is his goatee a problem? Probably not, but it has kept me up at night so you decide.

Cashier Took An Uncomfortably Long Time Handing Back Change

I tried to avoid paying with cash at all costs. It's too awkward too frequently. But whenever I'm shopping at a small business I switch to cash out of the goodness of my heart so they can avoid the credit card fees.

Then today, like most days, I got squeamish. When the purchase total comes to something like $1.97 I want to kill myself. It's physically painful. I'm captain loser on the SS Thrifty.

Why?

When there is a total around $1.97, 95% of the time the cashier will be out of pennies and will have to crack a new roll. Whenever this happens there will be at least 3 people behind me in line. And there is me, holding up the line because I'm waiting for 3 cents.

I don't really care for the 3 cents, but feel like a butthole saying:

"Oh, you can keep it."

"Really sir? Gee golly, you mean it? Wow, hold on a second. Hi honey, it's me. Set the champagne chilling, Ben said we can keep his three cents. I know, he's incredible. Handsome and generous is so rare to see these days."

This is the burden I face when trying to help out the small business by paying cash. Cash is not king. It makes you feel like a cheap peasant.

People think they can text and drive when they can't even drive. Why can't cashiers preemptively crack rolls of pennies? Instead I wait there with a stupid smirk on my face and do the sympathetic eyebrow lift when she looks up at me.

A penny saved, embarrassment accrued as interest.

The Escalator is Broken So I Have to Walk up It

After a laborious day of shopping, which included a gigantic orange julius, I lay my eyes upon a demoralizing sign: "Escalator broken. Sorry for the inconvenience."

Mustering a supernatural amount of strength and courage, I took the first step onto what was now stairs and made the momentous climb to the second level of the mall. The amount of calories exerted rivaled that of the funnel cake I had for lunch. Probably a wash on calories consumed vs. calories burned for the day.

I'm just another victim of a technically advanced society. Sometimes they dangle a carrot in front of you, then take it back right as you're about to chomp on it.

How long ago was it that Mitch Hedberg made the joke about an escalator being unable to breakdown, but only become stairs? Something this tragic, you can only laugh or cry. Mitch made us laugh, but reality will make you cry.

All I can do is hope my children can see a world without the exerting burden of stairs.

Drive Thru Lane was Backed Up So I Had To Go Inside Like a Peasant

95 degrees outside and I'm sweatier than the devil's arm pit. I have a mere 30 minutes to eat something for lunch before I have to head back to work.

On a day like this, I have only one option. To get myself a refreshing iced coffee and breakfast sandwich (for lunch) from a nearby coffee shop.

Upon arriving, I can't tell if I'm looking at the line for the drive thru or a really unenthusiastic parade. It's insane. At least 10 cars are in queue, slowly inching up in line.

I had no choice. My chariot came to a slow halt in front of the coffee shop and I stepped into the wild hot heat.

Unbearable.

Sweat began to foment on my forehead, like being struck by an invisible rain shower. I was forced to take at least 20-30 steps before being blown in the face by the cool breeze of the air conditioned coffee shop.

Serenity.

It was short lived, though. Two minutes later I was tossed back into the scorching Summer sun, burning my Norwegian skin into melanoma territory. It's the debt I pay society to not waste gas in the drive thru. You're welcome.

There Is a Shopping Cart In The One Open Parking Spot

Shopping centers are a conundrum for me. I hold the dual feelings of hating them, but also being fascinated.

As I drove toward the front of the parking lot at a pace that would have launched a careless toddler soaring like a Frisbee, I spotted an open space right near the entrance!

Car blocked.

I was expecting a smart car or a cute little VW Jetta, but this is an outrage.

A shopping cart.

One of the saddest sights of all humanity—wasted potential. I could have been in the store looking for a new internet connected TV, but I'm circling the lot again like an obese man waiting for the desert pizza to get refilled at the buffet.

What is the mentality of someone who just abandons the shopping cart? *"Well, groceries packed and loaded. I don't think I can walk 20 more feet to guide this baby to its home. I'm already sweating from loading the groceries and eating multiple samples. I'll just leave it here and some idiot will take care of it."* Then I apathetically drive past it, forced to do a few more loops around the bend.

America needs a social movement against people who abandon shopping carts. This is where the "See something. Say something." principle should come into effect. As far as I know, and I don't have any proof yet, but leprechauns aren't putting the shopping carts there. That means that real, visible people are doing it in plain daylight.

See a Cart, Have a Heart (and verbally shame whoever left it there).

That's the real slogan for a revolution.

Shopping Isn't Getting Better

Am I a masochist for shopping as much as I do?

Probably. Though, who isn't?

Shopping isn't a fun experience no matter if in-store or in my underwear online. While shopping in-store I'm stuck with whatever the price is. I don't have the endurance to drive all around town whittling the price down by $1.60. I take the price as is and deal with it.

When shopping online, there is always work to do. If I don't have an account, I have to create an account. Oh, a coupon code box? But I don't have a coupon. I'll spend the next 20 minutes searching the internet like an archaeologist looking for the obscure coupon code that's likely expired. Then before I can click "Complete Order" I have to do a quick search around the net to make sure I got the lowest price possible. What if I didn't? What if I'm overpaying by $2. I couldn't live happily knowing that.

All of this equates to much more effort than is reasonable. But allllll shopping is moving online. Woo…Just means more work for me. At least I can remain pantless. Hallelujah.

Shopping online just creates more work, which would be fine except I already work. And work is exhausting. Not the actual work, but all the collateral problems.

WORK

Welcome To The Working Week

We hear about the Nike sweatshops, the workers committing suicide at iPod factories, and the inhumane working conditions in India.

But what about corporate America? When do our problems get some ink? Is it so nice to be working in air conditioned offices while it's a beautiful day outside? Is it so fun to be overpaid for work you do, but don't derive meaning from? Is it a blast to become obese because we sit for 8 hours a day in soft chairs and pay for other people to make lunch for us?

These are the problems facing the average working American. It's not an easy job, but someone has to do it. What follows are a few of the problems I've personally faced working in corporate America. I have no doubt they resonate with others across the First World. For the most part we sit in silence, afraid to speak out. We take quiet comfort watching *The Office* and repeated showings of *Office Space* on TBS.

If anyone can offer these corporate jockeys a shoulder to cry on, it's me. I've been and lived in the cubicle farm. I've worked in offices that had the air conditioning on too high in the Summer and the heat too hot in Winter. Offices that had only tap water available. Offices without a vending machine. Offices without a cafeteria. I've paid my dues.

These are the First World Problems of the corporate world. Take solace and know that you're not alone in your 9 to 5 struggle, you cubicle monkey.

It's a Beautiful Day Outside But I Wouldn't Know It Since I'm Gainfully Employed

According to my iPad, it's a dazzling 80 degrees and sunny outside. It doesn't mention it, but I'm also inclined to believe that birds are chirping, kids are frolicking, and the homeless man with the violin on the street corner is playing Vivaldi's "Summer."

But I have no idea what it's like outside because I'm gainfully employed. It's terrible.

On walks to the water cooler, I can see the window with the sun shining. It looks magnificent. I bet all the unemployed people are at the beach just throwing a giant party.

This is when our boss is supposed to say, "Hey guys, it has been a long week. You kids go have some fun while you're young." I've only heard rumors of that happening at other offices, but never where I work.

Stuck.

We don't leave early. Sunrise to sunset. I could technically be a vampire and get through life without making that many sacrifices.

If you get work off on a nice day, send me a picture please. I want to know what the real world is like. You can be the Andy Dufresne to my Red from *The Shawshank Redemption*.

Get busy living for me.

People With Nalgenes Ruin Drinking Fountains

I'm a simple man. Most days I sit diligently at my computer, putting in 8 hours without much complaint or fuss.

During those 8 hours, I like to break up my day with a little walk down the hall to the drinking fountain.

Hurry up and wait.

Every single trip. No, I'm not exaggerating. OK, but only slightly. Every visit to the drinking fountain, I get stuck behind an IT turd filling up the 10-gallon Nalgene. Yes, you're saving landfills from non-combustible water bottles, but don't ram it down my dry throat.

What drives me insane is that when they go to fill up the Nalgenes, they are only half full. I have to wait 30 seconds in the drinking fountain line like I'm back in 3rd grade and just got thirsty during kickball.

You're not trekking in the Sahara Desert. You're not Bear Grylls. You're just someone who delicately sips water all day like a little kid who is afraid he's going to wet the bed. If someone approaches the water fountain let them cut instead of saying, "Just a minute. Sorry." while you basically fill an NFL-sized Gatorade bucket.

I'm not asking for much, America. Just don't fill your Nalgene to the brim if you can't drink it all.

My Work Lacks Meaning

Show up. Do Work. Get paid. Repeat.

Sounds like a great recipe for a decent life, but I feel somewhat empty inside. It's like eating cheesecake for dinner. Delicious, but unsatisfying if that's all you have.

So here I am, showing up for work day after day, entering data, getting paid, and living a life without meaning. Do people benefit from what I do? I have no idea. I'm not even entirely sure what I do. Just hit copy and paste a bunch? That sums it up.

It's only a matter of time before a robot or computer program takes my job. And why wouldn't they? It would be a blessing as far as I'm concerned, which isn't very far.

When your work lacks meaning, it's hard to care. When you don't care, you generally don't do a good job, which leads to getting fired.

My problem is that I don't care about my job, but I still do a good job so there is little chance I'll get fired.

I'm an optimist though. One day soon computers might be able to wipe out my entire department. Finally then, and likely only then, will I be forced to pursue something I love.

Viva la robots!

Forgot To Bring My Headphones To My Soul Deadening Job So I Must Buy New Ones At Lunch

For the last five minutes before leaving my apartment I've been in a frenzied panic. Like an amateur drug raid, I've been scouring my apartment for my one pair of headphones. They are nowhere.

Just yesterday I was listening to some Beastie Boys while on the way to work. Now everything I've come to know and love has been ripped away from me. I still have noise canceling head phones, but those are too intrusive for work. I've got nothing.

This is going to be the worst day of my life. I should take a sick day, right? Yeah, great idea except for the fact that I never get sick. My work would know something was up. My fault for proudly wearing on my sleeve the fact that I only get the sniffles once a year, tops. I also don't get paid time off, so that's never going to be an option.

Here is what I do on a daily basis: I hit CTRL+C on the computer. Then I hit CTRL+V. That's it. Copy and paste all day long. It's the worst job in the entire world except that I get to listen to my iPod. That was until I lost my headphones. Granted, I work right across the street from the largest mall in America, so I can and will get a new pair, but that isn't until lunch. 4 hours of silence about to ensue. Here is to humming the entire Beach Boys catalog.

I silently carry on. I have no other choice. But to work in silence like some sweatshop, occasionally having to converse with my coworkers. Time moves as if the clock was shot with a horse tranquilizer.

Today is the worst day of my working life since I forgot my mid-morning snack bar.

Too Much Cash In My Wallet To Fold It

After a long night of working my side job, I now have too much cash on hand to comfortably fit in my wallet. In my moonlighting gig, I work as a valet where at the end of the night I leave with a stripper-esque wad of cash.

Getting paid in cash can be incredibly frustrating on busy nights. I'm the type of guy who doesn't have a money clip and just prefers to carry all of my money in a leather wallet, classic style. But this is a problem when I have too much cash on hand, which happens often.

I can barely fold my wallet. When it's in my back pocket and I sit down I look like I have a gangster lean. It looks ridiculous and I'm sure it's wreaking havoc on my posture.

The only solution I have is to gratuitously spend money as fast as I can. This is even difficult though, since I'm so accustomed to buying everything on Amazon. And because I'm mostly tipped in one dollar bills, I look like a jerk if I buy anything expensive. "Gee, thanks pal. Take a nap while I count out $150 in ones, jerk."

Why not take all of the dollar bills to the bank to deposit? Because that's uncomfortable. Once I brought in about $250 in one dollar bills. The teller could barely make a questioning face before I could blurt out, "Sorry. I had a busy night stripping." Either she didn't realize I was joking or she didn't think it was funny. That was my last trip to the bank.

Mo' Money, Mo' Problems.

Ate Two Lunches And Now I Need a Nap

I need a wheel barrel stat! Just roll me around the office, down to the water fountain and vending machine, then tip me over at my desk.

This morning I decided to be a productive and active member of society, so I actually prepared a lunch. Made a turkey sandwich, with bacon and cheese. Even brought my own avocado. And because avocado is only good for a few hours, I had to put the entire behemoth on my sandwich. It was disgusting how good that sandwich was. Barely got in a breath before I was licking the last avocado blob off my arm.

Then a co-worker chimed into my office, "Hey, we're going to lunch at T.G.I. Friday's. Wanna come?" Ughhh…This doesn't happen very often, so I always feel compelled to say yes, even though I already ate. I dusted the crumbs off my shirt and piled into the car for Americas favorite generic restaurant chain.

As we sit down, I figure I'll get just a small appetizer or maybe side salad. Then I saw some new Mango Pineapple burger whose picture is food porn to my eyes. It was gluttonous love at first bite. Eating the Mango Pineapple burger was like experiencing the worst of Hawaii, which by Minnesota in January standards is pretty damn good.

By the end of the meal I came within an inch of having to unbutton my pants to give the belly a little bit of running room. Then I realized most of my coworkers were only half way done with their meals. I was in the awkward situation of having to "pretend" like I'm still eating, where if you look at me for three seconds, you'll see me picking up salt shavings and sipping on water like a mule. Thus, I essentially cleaned my plate twice.

I'm fat, full, and ready to mail it in the rest of the day.

Diarrhea On The Way Home From Work

This is the problem with America: While driving home from work and you happen to get stuck in rush hour while simultaneously getting diarrhea, you're screwed.

One solution would be to allow diarrhea-stricken schlubs to take the carpool lane. It's the humane thing to do. You see, if this was a third world country, I'd simply have pulled my cab or bicycle to the side of the road where I would have made a giant mess, next to a thousand messes. No judgment, no shame, just sweet relief.

This must be my punishment for moving to the suburbs and working in the city. The longer my commute, the more likely some unwanted variables will come into play.

It doesn't happen every day, which is precisely why something needs to be done about it. I have no idea when it will strike next, despite there being an extremely high correlation between diarrhea and me eating McDonald's hash browns. I'm no statistician though.

Write me in for President in the next election and I'll put the people with uncontrollable BMs on a porcelain throne.

That's a promise.

Always Healthy So I Never Get To Take a Sick Day

It's a beautiful day outside. And I'm stuck inside typing away, staring at a glowing monitor. Another horrible day of perfect health.

One of my biggest grievances with my body is that I never get sick.

Never.

At worst I get a bad case of the sniffles. That's it. How the hell am I supposed to stay at home, drink orange juice and watch Netflix all the stuffy day if I never get sick? I'd have to take a vacation day. I'm so popular for never getting sick that no one would ever believe that I was sick. Plus, I'm a terrible liar. I'd start by telling everyone I was going to see my doctor and end up singing Robert Palmer's "Bad Case of Loving You."

I guess I do have allergies, mainly via cats. Before work I could rub my face in some disgusting cat hair and show up with itchy eyes and a nose that runs with the endurance of a Nigerian marathoner.

My health problem is so bad that sometimes I find myself wishing I was sick. It's clearly not physically possible, but for once I'd like to know the taste of chicken noodle soup and bad daytime television. I can only read about how terrible *The View* is, but I've never experienced it!

Here I write, healthy as an ox. Wishing for just a sprinkling of sickness. Whooping cough or a sore throat so I could drink liquids. I'm pretty good at drinking liquids.

Here is to wishing I can be sick just one day in my life.

I Feel Wildly Uncomfortable When People Sing Happy Birthday To Me

This is why I hate my birthday. While I enjoy the gifts, the food, the cake, and the friends, I would trade all of that in a heartbeat if it meant people would never again gather around me and sing "Happy Birthday."

Part of celebrating someone's birthday is making them feel special. But the Happy Birthday song makes someone wish they were a turtle that could recede into their shell and never come out again.

Today is my birthday and I feel uncomfortable.

I was hoping it would just be another day at work and my birthday would go unnoticed, but thanks to Facebook that's impossible in our connected society. I can't fart without it showing up in someone's Newsfeed.

So toward the middle of the afternoon, while I was just plugging away building a website, a choir of coworkers circled my desk and in unison belted out some awkwardness. My first thought was, "Thank God it's cheesecake and not sheet cake." Sheet cake is a gesture cake. It shows you made an effort, but no one is really interested in actually eating it. I'd rather eat a bucket of communion wafers than sheet cake. I've documented the awfulness of sheet cake. The last birthday we celebrated at work, two squares of the giant sheet cake were eaten. The cake just sat in the break room for a month before someone finally put it out of its misery.

The problem with the Happy Birthday song boils down to this-the birthday (wo)man has no idea what to do while people are singing. You feel like a creep looking around at the other people awkwardly singing off-key. Just staring at the cake makes you feel like a fat pile of trash. Your eyes just wander around while you patiently wish for the song to be over.

The ideal work birthday for me goes like this: A coworker pops their head into my cubicle and says, "Hey Ben. We picked up some ice cream cake and pie for your birthday. It's sitting on the counter in the break room if you want any."

That is the perfect birthday. And the day I receive that birthday is the day I work from home.

Ban the "Reply All" Button Immediately, Please

There is a warm place in Hell reserved for people who hit "Reply All" to mass emails.

It takes brass balls or sheer stupidity to hit the God-forbidden "Reply All" button.

Yes, it's great that Susan is leaving her position for bigger and better things, but is it necessary, Todd, to let the entire department know that you're wishing her all the best? Is it? Were we all thinking to ourselves, "Hmm…Todd is on this email? Is he happy for Susan? How does he feel about this?" Do we care about you, Todd? Are we going to lose sleep at night if you don't respond? Do we need to know of your gratitude in regard to Susan's service of sitting at her desk and gabbing about her funny dog to coworkers for 10 consecutive years? Probably not.

But thanks for clearing the air, Todd. Now if you'll find the nearest empty elevator shaft to throw yourself down, we'd all appreciate it. Thanks! Sincerely, all of humanity.

Most of the time I'm not angry when someone hits Reply All to an email. I'm more so curious as to how they got their shirt on over their giant head.

Should I blame the people and their inflated egos who hit Reply All? Or should I blame Gmail, Outlook, Yahoo, and whoever else still hosts email?

The only Reply All that has even been appropriate contains one of the following messages:
- There are donuts in the break room.
- It's beautiful outside. Marketing can leave early.
- Free puppies in the lobby. Go get yourself one.

But that never happens. Never.

Ate Breakfast And Then a Coworker Brought In Bagels

When historians eventually examine my life to solve the question of "How did someone with so much potential amount to so little in life?" this will hold the answer.

Today, I made myself a man's breakfast. Extra thick bacon, prepared in the oven, married with three eggs over easy and a giant mug of coffee. There is something about making breakfast for yourself that is so satisfying. When you make breakfast first thing in the morning, you've already done something productive and it truly *feels* good.

And now I feel horrible.

After arriving to work with an ounce of pride in my step, I was alerted that a coworker brought in bagels and everyone could help themselves. The situation was exacerbated because I'm generally one of the first people in the office, which means I got the first pick of bagels.

I'm kind of full right now. Three eggs and three extra thick pieces of bacon can do that to you. But, I'm also exceptionally thrifty so I feel it's my duty to take advantage of free food whenever possible. In several cases this has led to hemorrhaging diarrhea, but my love for bagels trumps all.

Not wanting to be rude, I walked back to see what type of bagels we were dealing with. Dear Lord—two dozen bagels with untapped assorted cream cheeses to pick from. I felt slightly faint as my imagination danced with what sort of combination to make.

I picked the cinnamon bagel with strawberry cream cheese. A sophisticated choice for the workplace. While loading up my bagel, I discovered one of the finest things any human can experience, opening the lid of a cream cheese container, peeling back the plastic, and seeing an untapped canvas to work with. The simple joy a man can receive from skimming just the top of the mountain of cream cheese with the knife is really indescribable.

So I returned to my cubicle, ready to add a bagel to the bacon and eggs party in my stomach. T-minus 30 minutes until the party gets evicted.

I Have To Drive My Car To Work

Because I live in the suburbs and work in another suburb, I am rendered unable to use public transportation. It's awful. At least I think. I could just be thinking that the grass is always greener on the other side, when it turns out my first step to the other side would be into dog turds.

My desire to take public transportation doesn't stem from my love of the government or desire to support it. It entirely comes from being lazy. I can't afford a chauffeur, so my only other option is a crowdsourced chauffeur full of people who love to talk loudly on their cell phones.

Driving to work is exhausting. You have to put on pants, walk out the door, then stop and go, stop and go, repeat. Take your eyes off the road for half a second and you're a story on the local news.

I don't understand why we can't synchronize the freeway signs to say, "Everyone hit the gas in 3...2...1!" and the traffic jam would end. But it never ends. I'm perpetually stuck playing the kick drum on the brake pedal.

All I want from my commute to work is the ability to watch movies on Netflix and browse the internet on my iPad. Peanuts to ask for, really. I don't care if I'm next to an insane bum or a real estate agent looking to network my face off. I just want to relax for a few moments during my short, meaningless life, whose memory will be erased by the tides of history.

Driving my own car on my own schedule to work is making me miserable.

Don't Have An Office So I Can't Fart At Work

Let me first say that I love my day job. I love working for a small company where I basically have the freedom to implement any neat idea I have. With that said, I do have a slight beef.

I started my job with my own office. It wasn't anything too glamorous. Just a nice sized space with a solid desk that I could clutter with random papers and pistachio shells.

Then things got busy, we hired on some additional talent and I had to move offices. And there lies the rub—my days of passing gas at will are over.

In better times, I could sneak out a few coffee farts and if someone happened to dash into my office, I'd sniff it up before they could get wind of it.

But in today's workplace, I'm forced to bottle up my gas to the bursting point like a Coke can in a paint shaker. Society feeds us these gas-inducing foods like McGriddles, breakfast burritos and hot pockets, giant sugary coffee drinks, and bacon. Then we aren't supposed to emit any smell. It's not possible. Either you occasionally stink from the food or you smell like you've been coated in cheap cologne.

If we have "Smoking sections" at airports, restaurants, and a few buildings, why can't we have gas rooms? You could even combine it with the smoking room so things wouldn't get too weird. The smells would probably cancel each other out, right?

I constantly feel like if someone poked me with a needle, I would pop and fly around the room like a deflating balloon. Most days I'm so bottled up I could propel my way home from the office, just constantly hovering a few feet off the ground like I had on an invisible jetpack.

As for now, I'll keep using my traditional formula of crop dusting as

I walk through the accounting department. Then watch them turn on each other in blame like *Lord of the Flies*.

Stay gassy, America.

I'm Forced To Use Internet Explorer At Work

Do we work in an antique shop? Do we enjoy self-torture? No? This is against the Geneva Convention, right? Then why do we have to use Internet Explorer at work?

It's obviously intentional. The company wants to make the internet experience so painful in hopes that you'll avoid Facebook, YouTube, Twitter, and any other fun site. Therefore, they make the absolute worst browser in existence mandatory.

Internet Explorer is where fun goes to die on the internet. Internet Explorer is as compatible as Muammar Gaddafi. But the workplace loves it.

We don't even get the latest version of Internet Explorer. I think this is IE 8? Every time I want to open a new tab, I'm forced to open a new window. Impossible to multitask.

With Internet Explorer, every fancy and fun website looks like someone took a grenade to it. The spacing is off, alignment out of whack. Obviously the web developer didn't think he'd have people from 2003 checking out his website.

Being forced to use Internet Explorer is like being given just an appetizer plate for a buffet. There is so much out there to enjoy, but you can only experience a small fraction of it.

Why can't anyone write a good computer virus to kill Internet Explorer? Do everyone a favor and wipe out Internet Explorer from every single computer. The population at large will thank you.

90% Of People Work a Job They Hate

One of the worst things about working in the First World is that it's far too easy to take a job that you hate. Right now, if you stand up at your cubicle and look around, 90% of people you work with have an active dislike of their job or at best, they're indifferent.

In the Third World, even if you don't have a job that you're passionate about, you at least have sweat and dirt on your hands to show that you've accomplished something for the day.

When I spent 9 months doing data entry (Hitting control+c, then control+v), I had nothing to show for my work. I came home looking the same as when I left my crappy apartment that morning. For all my roommate knew, I could have been circling the block all day, putting up the facade of having an hourly job.

College burdens us with debt, which we have to start paying off almost right away. So then we do what college tells us to and take a "safe" job with steady pay and upward mobility! We tell ourselves that it's only temporary and we just need something stable while we find our dream job. But soon the regular paycheck becomes harder than heroin to quit, which makes everyone hate their job even more. They've become too dependent on a paycheck to quit. Eventually, they come to resent themselves for giving up on their dream.

These rants are for you, working man of America. Thanks for putting up with horrible managers, people who still send faxes, terrible coffee, and a job that you don't even like. But you do it for the better good of America. At least I think so?

BATHROOMS

The Devil's Dungeon

Can't spend half the book complaining about food without talking about the consequences. We're coming full circle, people. Keep up with me.

When it comes to public restrooms, one would expect we've come pretty far in America. The country that produced Larry Bird, Adam Lambert, and Bill Walton can surely handle their plumbing, right?

Bathrooms in America aren't much better than the poo pit the kid in *Slumdog Millionaire* falls into. Each bathroom is a war zone filled with the collateral damage of trash bins overflowing with paper towels, pools of water everywhere, and abandoned turds that no one considered flushing.

In a way, the name "restroom" is a misnomer. There is nothing relaxing or restful concerning restrooms. Instead of finding peace of mind, I'm holding my breath making sure I don't lean against the edge of the sink where water waits to get on my crotch. I try to get in and out like a bank robbery. This must be confusing for someone just learning English. "You mean people rest here? But how? Where? Why does it look like they destroyed their place of rest?"

Restrooms were bound to become a problem for the First World. When you glorify and obsess over food, simple math can tell you what the next problem will be. You can't pull the fire alarm and not expect a fire truck to show up.

So here we stand — restrooms out of control - a lawless sector of society where we are inches from flinging feces like monkeys. Where anarchy rules. A place to be feared and avoided at all costs.

This is the First World and the problems we face in the restroom.

Public Restrooms Are Disgusting

A lot of people wonder why public bathrooms are so disgusting. Well, considering no one *really* wants to use a public restroom, the only people who use them are those who *have* to use them. Oh, and old people use them. Today, while at a giant shopping mall, I witnessed the second old man I've seen pooping with the stall door open. I just turned around like I stumbled on a dead body in the woods.

Public restrooms are similar to prostitutes. They're an absolute last resort. No one wants to use one, but in times of desperation after every possible option has been exhausted, they'll be waiting for you at the bottom. They're no one's first option and you never tell someone you're going to use one. They're the last refuge of a man (women don't poop) who has exercised every other possible option.

Everything comes back to food. Look around at the food options at your average mall. 100 to 1 ratio of greasy food to healthy food. When you're brewing a burrito with popcorn, frozen yogurt, and other miscellaneous treats in your stomach, nothing human can come from that. It's going to be a mess shared with the public.

All of this is the perfect recipe for total anarchy in the bathroom. It's only used out of desperation. No one wants to be there. Everyone is in a hurry. And anything goes.

The Splash Guard Didn't Protect the Splash

Modern day bathrooms are a stinky collage of barbarism and technology. From pig troughs to urinal dividers and auto-flushing-terminator toilets. In Third World countries, bathroom problems don't exist. The bathroom is wherever you drop your pants or a giant hole in the ground.

In America, we have to complicate things by having different sets of rules and equipment scattered about. Public bathrooms basically reflect the tax code. Depending on where you are and who you are makes a big difference.

The two basic urinals:
Basic (w/o splash guard):
When I use the standard urinal, I always go for the kids' urinal. It's not as creepy as it sounds. I just like feeling super tall like an NBA player. What's wrong with that? Nothing to complain about there.

Basic (with Splash Guard):
I love splash guards, but sadly they don't seem to exist. "What? I've seen them!" What you've seen is a faux splash guard. It doesn't actually do anything, much like France's army. I learned this while I was at a baseball game.

As I emptied the gas tank, I felt a slight dusting of urine on my toes (yeah, wearing sandals is a terrible idea…). I shrugged it off as a minor disturbance, until I realized that it continued as I was buckling my belt. The little tyke next to me unleashed a firehouse of human lemonade onto my now saturated sandals.

The problem with splash guards is that they don't extend to the ground. Instead all they do is block the sausage cam. The splash guard might as well be placed at eye level, since that's the only use it has.

No more half measures or half splash guards in America. This shouldn't give confidence to anyone who wants to build a wall along the Mexico border. We can't even keep pee off our feet. How are we going to block an entire country?

I Have To Use a Public Restroom Where I Pee In a Trough Like An Animal

The trough is fascinating. Who invented it? Really. What communist saw all of the individual urinals and thought, "No, I won't have this. We shall urinate as one!" So he birthed the troff urinal and now all men have to line up and pee in harmony.

Where did the idea for the trough urinal come from? "Hey, it works for fattening up pigs. Let's have a bunch of dudes whiz into it."

It's highly efficient, but that doesn't make it right. Death squads were also efficient, but we don't still have those.

Is there no alternative to the trough? At least provide a TV or something to look at. Maybe that's how you get kids to read these days. In class, fill them up with glass of water after glass of water. Then when they visit the trough, the teacher's lesson plan is the only thing to read at eye level. We'd become a factory producing baby geniuses.

But today we urinate at the trough like an animal with nothing to look at except bricks. We aren't animals, most of us anyway.

Free Toilet Paper Isn't Free

If I know one thing about life, it's that free toilet paper isn't free.

When you step into a public restroom to use their facilities, as I did this afternoon, the "free" toilet paper you use ain't free. No, you don't pay a monetary fee to use it. But it's guaranteed to take a tax on your colon and general comfort.

This is what the suits in Washington need to focus on. We waste so much tax money each year, why not at least grant us a mandate on double ply toilet paper in public restrooms? That's all I ask for.

Society is moving in two opposite directions. Public restroom toilet paper is getting thinner and thinner. At the same time, Americans are getting fatter and fatter, which of course means bigger turds.

It's as if we are being mocked each time we sit on the throne. "Take a deuce, buddy. Enjoy the scathing touch of what's basically sandpaper," the toilet paper heckles.

As a society, wouldn't we say this is a regression? We have 3D TVs, but we can't adequately provide toilet paper that isn't above the level of plywood? If it keeps getting worse, I'm going to eventually carry around my own toilet paper with me. Maybe that's what fanny packs are really for? They just hit the market too early so they were mocked, but now they serve more purpose than ever.

The night ended with a cold shower courtesy of a Chinese buffet and public restroom. My body paid heavily for that "free" toilet paper.

I Was Falsely Accused Of Stinking Up The Bathroom

No one is safe in the public restroom. Not even the innocent bystander who just drank too much loose leaf green tea and has the bladder of an infant.

While walking into the bathroom I stepped into a fog of nauseous fumes. It was so bad you could smell it from the hallway. But 30 minutes ago I drank a giant mug of green tea so I didn't have much of a choice, except to hold my breath and hope for the flow of a fire hose.

The silent stinker flushed the toilet and had the gall to not even wait for me to finish and leave so he could remain anonymous. He didn't mind branding this on his resume. Shocking that such a profane smell could come from such a small man.

As I walked out of the bathroom, a coworker walked right by on her way to the drinking fountain. She gave a small cough as she passed the bathroom, obviously choking on the man's foul smell. But with her math she saw someone leaving the bathroom and an abominable smell coming from the bathroom, so who do you think got blamed?

I have no idea if she harbors any ill will, but I've been paranoid ever since.

A Low Flow Toilet Ruined My Night

One comes to expect certain things in life: the opportunity to earn a decent living, protective yet not overbearing government, and the calm peace of knowing the toilet will properly flush while your wife is sleeping.

That was too much to ask.

After a long day of piling on coffee and fiber, the time came to make a deposit. Unbeknown to me, my body was at the bursting point. The town had been evacuated and the volcano was ready to erupt.

I silently took a seat at the porcelain throne as my wife slept soundly in the next room. After I became three pounds lighter I casually flushed, picked up my book, and prepared for bed. Except I noticed that the water came close to the brim, but didn't overflow. Odd. So, like any rational, tired man, I waited for the water to return to normal resting level and I gave another flush.

Like the wall of a dam breaking, the water rose uncontrollably until I was standing in a puddle of strawberries! ("Strawberries" is a euphemism for poo water. Sorry if this is your lunch break). It's 12:05am on a work night and I'm swimming against the current in turd creek. I grabbed the paper towels to pitifully slop up the mess.

This truly is pathetic. Not on my part. Society, is at fault once again. You can't continuously build bigger portions while at the same time strangling the water pressure of toilets. The only rationale to this is that there is some Wizard of Oz like evil overlord deep within government laughing maniacally, shouting, "Eat. Eat it up, America. Good luck flushing! Mwuaahaha!" Either that or plunger lobbyists are much stronger than people realize.

Whatever the case, America has lost and I need new socks.

Forgot To Bring My iPad To The Bathroom And Now I'm Bored

Like leaving for a road trip and bringing the personal DVD player, but forgetting to bring a DVD, I went to the bathroom and forgot my iPad.

It was too late to turn back. Before I realized my colossal error, my trow was dropped and the gears on the brown locomotive were already in motion.

As I sat in utter boredom beyond comprehension for at least 5 minutes, possibly as long as 7, I couldn't help but think of all the things I was missing out on...Playing *Angry Birds* on the giant iPad screen, browsing Tumblr, playing *Words With Friends*. I'm stuck basking in my own filth with nothing, but my tormented thoughts.

I'm rendered unable to carpe diem my crap. I can't even remember bowel movements before smart phones. Did they exist? I think I read magazines. I wonder what people did before Gutenberg? I guess they were probably outside then, so they were trying to not get eaten by a deadly mosquito or wild boar. I have no boar to fear except bore.

With a final flush, my time in isolation is over. Flushed away 7 minutes without entertaining myself.

Paper Towels Everywhere

There isn't a winning strategy to drying your hands in a public restroom.

None.

At home, you have the leisure of using a soft towel. In a public restroom, you've got the following options:
- Paper towels
- Vent
- Pants
- None of the above because washing your hands is for the bourgeois

Vents don't work because the human race hasn't discovered the Fountain of Youth. Therefore, we'd all die before our hands were dry. When using the wind power of a toddler blowing out their birthday candles, you might as well not even bother with the "high tech" machine.

Drying your hands on your pants is a valid option except it makes you feel weird. It's easier to pass off if you're wearing jeans, but what if you're wearing khakis? Do you want to risk having your butt look like it's been sweating profusely in the bathroom? Yahtzee.

Choosing to not wash your hands is too bold for my blood. Would I get sick from not washing my hands? Probably not. But you never know who is in the bathroom and how much they're judging.

So the only realistic option is to use paper towels. But that creates a mess. In 9 out of 10 bathrooms, there are paper towels stacked to the brim of the waste basket at all times. It's a poor man's version of Jenga you have to play in order to get your crumbled paper towel on top of the stack without it falling amongst the heap on the floor. It's not half as fun as it sounds.

Just once I'd like to see an empty trash can in a public restroom. That's all. But maybe I've just had consistently horrible timing for the last 25 years of my life.

Not With a Bang But a Flush

The future doesn't look good for bathrooms.

In many aspects of the public restroom, it seems that we keep regressing. We do away with the paper towels, only to replace them with machines that just make your hands cold and don't actually dry them.

The automatic flushers mostly just give your butt a shower. Half the time there will still be a present greeting me, which is hard to explain. Do ghosts exist? I'm not sure anymore.

Washing your hands only become more difficult. Half the restrooms have sinks with a little button to press for water that only lasts half a second. You have to wash one hand at a time or have a quicker draw than John Wayne. No wonder no one wants to wash their hands. You look like a fool.

Technology advances, the bathroom retreats. The world inches toward *Minority Report* while the bathroom retreats into the cave. It's a mess and will continue to be for the foreseeable future.

Until the public restroom is no longer composed of urinal troughs, mountains of paper towels, low flow toilets, and single ply toilet paper—I'll have a mission to be on.

America needs better public restrooms and I'm going to make it happen.

RANDOM

Random First World Problems

There are some problems that simply cannot be defined by a certain chapter or class, but the wounds cut just as deep.

A shish kebob of problems stack up each day. Fluffy pillows, Facebook awkwardness, Twitter being down when I want to live tweet my lunch, and the clustering baggage that comes with college and no responsibility.

This is the home for the homeless First World Problems. Read on to feel the pain.

I Forgot To Consider The Environment Before Printing An Email

That's it for me. Might as well sell my house, all my possessions, and get on the first red eye to Vegas, where anything goes. I've just committed the cardinal sin—I forgot to consider the environment before printing an email.

I feel the burden of failing all of society. What's become of me? In high school I only received one detention and that was due to being 3 minutes tardy because I couldn't start my day without a McGriddle from McDonald's. That's it. My entire record.

But today there is no turning back. I do not seek, nor do I expect forgiveness from society. I know the wrongs that I have committed.

How many trees must die at the hands of my carelessness? Dare I walk into a forest for they now know my name? There walks Ben printing like paper grows on trees.

Is there any solace in the fact that what I printed was a hilarious picture of an LOL Cat? There are currently no cats in the office and someone sent me the picture in a forward. The decision to print it off and hang it on the wall was so obvious I didn't think for a modicum of a second about the environment.

Somewhere in a quiet forest, Al Gore is applying 20 lashes to his bare back for my inconsiderate actions.

All I See On Facebook Is Baby Pictures

I hate Facebook. It's the worst.

What used to be a place to see funny links from friends, insane ramblings from the same three girls, and to manically poke people has turned into a wasteland of cute.

All I see on Facebook is baby pictures.

Everywhere.

Overnight, Facebook has become a place for all of my "friends" to life-log their kids inane activities—Tommy took a poo poo. Tommy won't nap. Tommy just hiccuped. Tommy is crawling so fast. He's going to be a track star!

Stop it, please.

What makes this worse is that most of my friends are now the age where they are having legitimate children. Their baby making has spread like a disease. Little burping, pooping, and crying zombies have been tyrannizing my Newsfeed.

When did Facebook turn from the place to mock your friends for puking all night to complain about your baby spitting up all night?

All Facebook needs is a baby filter. Block out all babies, except those that are directly related to me. Thanks in advance, Zuck.

The Neti Pot Is Self-Torture

Allergies aren't real. They are simply a weakened mental state of mind. This doesn't stop me from sneezing every time I'm around my parent's dog. Though, correlation isn't necessarily causation. Of course, the only solution for my stuffed beak is the Neti Pot—the First World's self-inflicted torture device.

The Neti Pot is a fascinating invention. Shaped like a plastic genie lamp, it magically clears your schnoz of any blockage through what is essentially self-waterboarding. I haven't technically been waterboarded, but I realize it's not a trip to pleasure-town.

But one can't deny if you go into getting waterboarded with a blower full of snot, it's not a complete loss. You'll at least leave the torture session breathing like a champ. There's a positive to everything.

If the terrorists ever take me alive, I'll probably need a good waterboarding since I'm "allergic" to dust, which stale caves are full of.

Until then, I'll keep Neti-Potting / Waterboarding myself. I just hope that while using the Neti Pot, I don't spill any secrets or confess to any war crimes. Isn't that side effect? I'll keep you posted, America.

Late To Work Because I Was Stuck Behind a Bus On The Tracks

Whenever I'm running late, God throws a bus in front of me and a set of train tracks.

No one on planet Earth understands why busses stop before train tracks and open their doors. Is it so they can hear if a train is coming? You would think that would be it, but that doesn't make sense. If that is the safest thing to do, why does no one else do it?

I can also personally guarantee that bus drivers don't do this while driving home. They don't stop before the tracks in their Dodge Stratus, pop the door and listen for a whistle.

If everyone did this, it would simply slow society to a slug's crawl. Everything would just shut down.

It's as if they are expecting to stop short of the tracks and see a train blowing by with Keanu Reeves hanging out a boxcar screaming, "Get out of the way! The terrorists cut the brakes!" If that actually did happen, you'd never hear me complain about anything ever again.

But until we see an out of control locomotive heading for a playground at recess, let's keep pace with the rest of society, bus drivers.

Have To Drive Across The State Border To Get Actual Fireworks

All I want right now is a box of Roman candles. That's all. I'm just an American man who wants to celebrate the birth of his country by sending colorful balls of fire into the air. But because the state of Minnesota believes that you shouldn't be able to light more than a match, I have to drive to Wisconsin.

To exercise my patriotic duty and reenact Nicholas Cage via *The Rock* on his knees sending up flares (look it up on YouTube), I had to invest an hour and a half, plus gas money to get to Hudson, WI and back.

Not sure what the logic was behind the state of Minnesota's decision to ban all the cool fireworks. "But congressman, Wisconsin has all the fireworks we are banning. Won't people just drive across the border?" "Wisconsin isn't a destination. It's a drive through state for people trying to get to the beautiful ponds and lakes of Minnesota."

And just like that I have to waste an entire Saturday driving to buy fireworks. All men may have been created equal, but we don't have equal opportunity to fireworks.

This would never fly in China. They've got fireworks that could send Kim Kardashian to the moon. Wait a minute…

I've got my fireworks now. Not going to lie, my blood pressure rose a little bit when I was crossing back over the border with $100 worth of fireworks. Felt the thrill of a drug smuggler. Though, it could have been the cheese curds I had for lunch kicking in, too.

Nightly News Is Boring

If you were to hand me a survey that asked, "How often do you watch the nightly news?" without hesitating, I would check "Seldom to never." Probably due to my love of not depressing myself before trying to sleep.

It's hard to not get depressed when watching the news. Local news is 60% who got raped / murdered, 10% weather with a guy walking outside into the elements Discovery Channel style, 5% sports, and then they sprinkle in a squirrel water skiing at the end for levity. With all of the soul-deadening news making you feel so empty and pessimistic, they suddenly shift gears over to "Hey, here is something someone uploaded on YouTube."

After the local news, you're supposed to click off the TV (or Clap-off if you're wise to that product like me) and expect the ZZZZZ's to fly out the window.

It doesn't happen. You toss and turn with ghastly thoughts of Mrs. Cunningham, whom you just met on TV, being mugged and beaten within an inch of her life. Heartwarming stuff.

This is why I don't watch the local news. I have no idea who was murdered today or which high school team won the state championship, but I'm happy. Except of course for all of my other problems.

Regrettably Threw All My Change Into The Wishing Well At The Mall

Having spare change on you is like having a collection of mini anvils in your pants weighing you down. I inevitably feel like an old man, reaching into my pockets to jingle around my car keys and spare change.

To someone from a third world country, wishing wells have to be one of the most puzzling enigmas on earth. Right up there with food fights and anorexia. If you take someone from Africa or India, where they walk three miles uphill both ways though land mine infested hills for a bucket of dirty water from a corrupt government well, and teleport them to the Mall of America next to the wishing well I'm looking at right now, their head would explode.

"Wa...Wa...Water!? Flowing out of clay man's mouth?! Must drink...Wha..No?!...What is this? Money?! Money everywhere! A miracle!"

Shock and awe. How could they waste this water? But wait, there is money! You could feed a family of eight in Mexico for a year with what you find in the average wishing well.

I hate throwing my change into the wishing well, but I loathe having coins in my pocket more. Perpetually unhappy until the only coins in this world are made of chocolate.

Favorite Indie Band Is Becoming Too Successful

People ruin everything.

Remember that. The more people enjoy something, the less happiness it brings me.

Who still likes the movie *Napoleon Dynamite*? No one. It won't be funny for at least another 5 years. People ruined it. They ruin everything. They latch onto something a few people enjoy and pound the fun out of it. I saw that movie while it was in only one theater in our entire state. Three months later, I couldn't go a day without someone bastardizing, "Your Mom goes to college."

Occasionally a great movie I love will remain at the cult level. FUBAR hasn't been ruined yet, but because I love it, it's inevitable that society will eventually drain all enjoyment from it.

The only thing I hold sacred in life is music. I live to find new music before other people so I can discover artists that aren't overplayed on the radio…yet.

And here is the problem.

One of my favorite bands, Peter Wolf Crier, is becoming too successful. They've been getting press / reviews in Pitchfork, The A.V. Club, and they were the CD of The Week at our local indie station, The Current. With their new album, they've been generating a lot of press and even selling out shows.

This is horrible news.

I don't want anyone else to be listening to them. I've had too many other things ruined in my life. Let me hold onto this one little band, with the care of Lenny from *Of Mice and Men*.

No one needs to know about the sweet harmonies they create. Let's just keep that a little secret between you and me…and whoever you tell because you probably can't keep a secret. Don't ruin this for me, society. You've done enough damage.

Pump the breaks, guys. Don't let society wreck your music just yet.

And step off, Seacrest.

First World Riots

We're Desperate to Riot in the First World.

We have no idea what we're doing with riots, do we?

As I write this, students at Penn State are taking to the streets to riot about the firing of a coach who knew about someone molesting a child, but kept them on staff. Penn State students reacted by rioting and flipping a TV station van, respectively.

How do we celebrate a home team championship victory? By destroying our own city, obviously. You can only high five so many people before your hands are itching to throw Molotov cocktails at police.

Age of retirement getting pushed back two years? Better riot. Have to pay back college loans I agreed to pay? Riot, man! Tuition increasing for college that I voluntarily chose to go to? Get me my best riot rocks, now! Won the Stanly Cup and I don't even care about hockey? If I'm not flipping a cop car in the next 30 minutes, I'm going to freak out.

All we see on cable news in the First World is people rioting in the Third World. We can barely think, "Ooh, fun!" before we are daring police to shoot us with tear gas. They may be rioting against a corrupt government holding their food shipment hostage, but that doesn't mean we can't riot out of solidarity when public union pensions are threatened to be cut.

When it comes to rioting, America and Europe are like that friend who tags along when everyone else knows they don't belong there. It's embarrassing, America.

Let's find something a little bit more riot worthy, like hotel beds.

Hotel Bed That I Paid To Sleep In Is Less Comfortable Than My Bed At Home

Typing this right now takes a massive feat of strength. I feel like Road Runner's anvil fell on my back while sleeping last night.

Being a considerate husband, I decided to go all out for the first wedding anniversary with my wife. I booked a room at a Holiday Inn in a suburb a good 15 minutes away from us. Yes, it even included the continental breakfast, which I believe is French for "Eat as many waffles as you can make." The room was mint.

After a delightful meal at Applebee's, we retired back to the room. Nine hours later I awoke feeling like an ancient Pharaoh resurrected from the dead by Brendan Fraser. The hotel bed, which I paid to sleep on, pile-drived (or is it pile-drove?) my back.

This is another burden of living in America. Most hotels can't keep pace with the comfort of home. They know you're only in town one night and one night only. Might as well destroy your back. Hotels already do this to your wallet, by taxing exorbitant fees.

If you can't match the quality of my bed at home, why even try? I'm already tormented with thoughts of what might have took place before me at most hotels. When there is no difference in quality of sleep between the bed and the floor, we are failing as a society.

Let's make an effort, hotels of America. Sleeping is the only thing people care about, but it's what you're worst at. When you try to please everyone, you please no one, which is what has happened with beds in hotels across America. The immediate remedy is to make a bed fit to my specifications. It may take the rest of America some time to adjust, but it is what's best for everyone.

I Really Want To See The New Independent Movie But It's Not Showing In My Theater

I'm somewhat of an aspiring movie aficionado. And naturally, most of my favorite movies are independent ones that either make you think or make you laugh without cheap physical humor.

The movie *Cyrus* is opening in dozens of theaters this weekend, but only on the coasts. The Midwest won't see the movie for at least another month. It's almost like Fox Searchlight doesn't realize how big of a fan I am. Here I want to support independent movies, but have to wait because I live in the heartland. Don't they realize that we don't have anything else to do, but mindlessly entertain ourselves?

When it comes to meaningless things like running for president, everyone heads to Iowa first, but important things like independent movies? We get them last. It's a damn shame. Do they expect me to see *Transformers* or the 8th *Spiderman* movie? I'm afraid my mind would melt if I did. I'd have to watch a marathon of Wes Anderson movies for a month and a half straight to make up for it.

If anyone needs independent movies first, it's the Midwest. New York and LA have plenty of other things to keep them busy, like non-chain restaurants and sunshine. Let us in the Midwest just have this one treasure. That's all I'm asking.

Didn't Get An Easter Basket This Year

The end of an era, I suppose. At the age of 25, I returned home to my parent's house to find out that I didn't receive an Easter basket this year.

Yes, I may be past the age of it being socially acceptable to receive an Easter basket, but it didn't have to stop this year. It's not like all of the sudden I stopped liking candy and the thrill of finding a plastic egg full of Reese's cups behind a couch cushion.

Instead, my parents finally hung up their cleats for good. Maybe it's degrading for them to pick out candy and hide it around the house? But when you see how happy it can make someone, isn't that what makes it worth it? Or maybe they think I'm getting fat. If that was the case, the defense would have a hell of a case to make.

When I become a parent of the luckiest kids in the world, I don't see myself ever stopping the tradition of hiding the Easter basket and candy. Unless my kids refuse to share their candy. Then the Easter bunny might take a little vacation.

During a Group Picture I Was Closest To The Camera So I Look Like a Giant

What a beautiful day at work. Besides the whole company being taken to my favorite sandwich shop of all time, the boss paid for it. It's now five hours later and I'm still full from the roast beef sandwich. But it wasn't all sunshine and milkshakes.

The group picture is an infestation of awkward and it needs to stop.

When I picked my seat at the giant booth that accompanied 6 other coworkers I didn't know I'd be choosing to be framed as an Ogre the rest of my life.

Since I was such a gentleman and let all of the ladies order before me, I took the last seat at the table which happened to be right on the end. Toward the end of the meal, one of the ladies thought it appropriate to take a photo to encapsulate either the roast beef or the bonding of the employees. Not sure which.

No big deal, I thought. Pretty sure I didn't blink during the picture. No beef in my teeth. No milkshake where my mustache would be. Should be alright. Then comes the Facebook notification.

You've seen this a million times, but you never think it will happen to you. I was a victim of the horseshoe group picture. Being just a few feet from the camera, I look like Shrek's albino step-child. Huge awkward head taking up the same amount of space as a whole employee in the back.

What makes it worse is that the guy on the other end of this ridiculous horseshoe is about 5 feet tall, tops. So he looks proportional compared to everyone else. And I'm the 6'1" troll.

We have cameras that correct for red eye, can countdown from 5, go underwater, and do just about anything except make you look normal in a group setting. Someone always gets burned, just like wedding photos.

A current trend in wedding photos is to take a group shot of everyone jumping. Guaranteed that someone has cement shoes that day. Doesn't matter if she is the skinniest person in the group, if she has bad timing everyone will think of her as the chubby marshmallow with no vertical.

Our society bans smoking within 25 feet of a building. We should ban photographs within 25 feet of a group. That way everyone can look proportional and a little bit grainy. Oh, in a perfect world…

Searched YouTube For Inspiring Speech. Watched 2 Hours Of Funny Cat Videos Instead

Looking for inspiration, I turned to YouTube for a dose of motivation.

Falling back on old reliable, I searched for Gary Vaynerchuk's Web 2.0 talk. Just a few minutes into it, I was feeling pretty confident and ready to hustle all night.

Then I remembered a coworker telling me about the Keyboard Cat meme. I thought I'd just open a new tab and keep the Gary Vayernchuk motivation going.

Keyboard Cat and Carmen San Diego? Too good.

I paused the Gary Vaynerchuk talk to watch the short minute and a half clip. Just a classic video made for YouTube. Then off to the side I see Keyboard Cat on Judge Judy—how can you *not* watch that?

Two hours later I'm watching a video of Ric Flair accusing The Macho Man of grabbing a fist full of trunks. I have no idea how I stumbled upon '90s wrestling videos, but I'm here now and loving it.

What am I doing on YouTube?

If the FBI ever raided my home, took me downtown, and searched the history on my computer—from YouTube alone they would consider me certifiably nuts. "He went from watching a dog skateboarding to a video of a large woman singing about sitting on the toilet to clips of Cheers. It makes no sense. He's ADD on steroids."

In fact, I think 99% of the population would be diagnosed with ADD after spending 30 minutes on YouTube. It's an endless rabbit hole filled with cats and crazy people, though often both.

No idea what I originally came to YouTube for, but thanks for the cat videos guys.

Graduated College And Learned Nothing

So long and thanks for the 100k in student loans!

0% of my income so far can be credited towards my college degree. Sure, I've worked luxurious jobs since graduating, such as: valet, vacuum salesman, data entry, car cleaner, and a temporary tattoo artist at the State Fair for Wal-Mart. (It was only for a day, but still a job.)

Going to college is necessary for some people—doctors, lawyers, anyone in the sciences. But for business? No. Not at all. How much can you learn about working in business from a 1980's case study on why New Coke failed?

When the list of what-you-need-to-know-to-be-successful-in-business-but-didn't-learn-in-college is longer than the list of what you learned in college, there is a huge problem.

Did I learn negotiation? Did I learn about sales or more specifically, how to sell my abilities (besides my devilishly good looks)? Did I learn how to network online? Did I learn about personal branding? Did I learn what to do when a customer destroys your business plan like a puppy home alone with a new sofa?

No!

When immigrants go to college in America and then return home, they're treated like royalty. When Americans graduate college, they're first in line for a barista job at Starbucks. College used to thin out the herd and graduate people prepared to jump right into a career. Now, any chotch willing to sign up for $100k in loans can get a degree and learn nothing about real life.

So college, thanks for, uh…the four year break from reality? Sorry, my minimum wage job (plus tips!) is beckoning.

I Hate Myself For Being Conscious Of a Family That Shall Not Be Named

In "Outliers: The Story of Success," by Malcolm Gladwell, we learn about plane crashes and what made one Korean airliner a failure. Part of the problem was cultural and the other part took multiple things going wrong.

The Family That Shall Not Be Named is Americas Korean plane crash.

20 years ago, we'd have no idea who a certain "celebrity" is. She'd be working at a PR agency in Los Angeles, married to a lawyer and complaining about how stuck up her neighbors are.

But today we're shoveled the Family That Shall Not Be Named by the butt load. Do I care about her wedding? Do I care about her divorce? Do I care about her birthday party in Vegas? No, but I know about it.

She made a sex tape at exactly the right time. 5 years later and no one would have cared. Her only job would have been holding a brief case on the show *Deal or No Deal*. 5 years earlier and her name wouldn't have made it out of the "18 and older" section of the video store, guarded by a mysterious curtain.

I'm undecided if it's a sign that we have things so great in America that we pay attention to someone so trivial or if we hate ourselves so badly that we're begging for anyone else to self-destruct.

The only respectable member of The Family That Shall Not Be Named is the Dad and he doesn't even carry the family name. The dude loves remote control helicopters more than life itself. I'd fly a miniature Black Hawk with him any day.

But instead of flying helicopters, more and more of my day is consumed by the Family That Shall Not Be Named. Taking over Miami. Taking over New York. Taking over Taking Over. Society has no idea why they care about the Family That Shall Not Be Named but they do.

If we are going to have to keep up with the Family That Shall Not Be Named, can we at least put them on *Fear Factor* or *Jeopardy*? Something with more drama than wearing the wrong outfit.

It's sad how much I know about the Family That Shall Not Be Named. If I ever lose my memory entirely, it won't be a complete loss.

The Pillows Are Too Damn Fluffy I Can't Take It Anymore

I'm mad as hell and I'm not going to take it anymore.

Because my wife has the crazy idea that I have allergies (the only things I'm allergic to are losing and turkey bacon), she purchased me a hypoallergenic feather pillow.

All would be well in the world and I'd be counting sheep, sawing logs, and catching Z's except that the pillow is too damn fluffy. I don't see how this pillow is practical for sleeping on. Probably because it isn't practical for sleeping on. It's a nightmare. The only use I see for it is decoration or smothering someone to death in their sleep. It would be perfect for that. The jury might even let you off light since you used a hypoallergenic feather pillow.

The ideal angle for the neck on a pillow is about 25 degrees. With this puffy pillow, I'm swimming in the 70 degree angle zone. How long before I drown in a flock of feathers? I'm not positive, but I am certain this will take years off of my life, all because I tried to experience a little comfort while resting.

Now my only hope for resting in peace is when I'm dead. Unless, I'm buried with a fluffy pillow. Dammit.

THE END OF THE ROAD

Time To Say Goodbye

This is the end, but it isn't the end. Tomorrow I'm going to wake up to a world that doesn't adequately stock its buffets, has confused old people in the self-checkout line, and produces pillows that are unreasonably fluffy. The problems will never end, but the book has to at some point or else it'd be called a blog.

I know you're thinking, "How can this be the end? He didn't even mention the Snuggie or Snookie?" My problems are just rain drops in the ocean of First World Problems. There will always be people who are limited to only taking out $300 from an ATM per day, have auto-correct on the iPhone forcing awkward conversations, and suffer near exhaustion while planning luxurious vacations.

Thank you for reading this collection of rants and ramblings. It wasn't easy to bear my soul and share all of the problems and pain I face on a daily basis. It got emotional during the food chapter. It's a difficult life, only owning a 42 inch LED internet-connected television, when so much more exists. But thanks for understanding my pain.

So, this is the actual end of the book. We're not going to go through a "You turn the final page" "No, you turn the final page" fight, though it would be adorable.

If you loved this book, write me at least a mediocre review on Amazon.com. The more reviews, the more books that are sold. The more books sold, the sooner I can do a cross-country tour, stocking public restrooms with double ply toilet paper like I'm Santa.

Make it happen, America (and Canada if it's not too much work).

You're Still Reading?

Oh, hi!

You're the person who stays in the theater while the credits are rolling after the movie, hoping for a bonus scene at the end.

Well, this isn't really a bonus clip.

But I just couldn't let it end.

Where do we go from here?

If you want to contact me, you obviously take the information below and act on it. Please send gifts of bacon and popcorn. That is all I want.

Email:
Hi@bennesvig.com

In Person:
Visit the Taco Bell Drive-thru on 394 and Louisiana in St. Louis Park, MN between 5:10pm-5:30pm every weekday and look for the unshaven man shouting for a Crunch Wrap Supreme.

Twitter:
@BenNesvig

Twitter Hashtag:
Tweet your First World Problems Review:
#FirstWorldProblemsBook

Reviews on Amazon:
On my computer I have a living document divided into two categories: With Us and Against Us.

When the world slips into chaos, which it will, you will want to be on the "With Us" column. Zombie uprising, invasion from Canada, nuclear winter, the apocalypse, or another season of *Jersey Shore*.

Any of those scenarios could mean the end of the world. When that happens you'll want to be "With Us" on my side. Trust me. I may not be very spry, but I'm crafty. I'm not afraid to throw sand and rake the eyes.

How can you join my team?

Leave a review on Amazon (whether positive or negative or extremely positive) and tweet me the link: @BenNesvig

This is officially the end. That's it. That's all. Thanks for reading / skimming this book. You could have played *Words With Friends* or read something that would have made you smarter, but you chose to spend your precious time with me and I appreciate that. You're the best.

ABOUT THE AUTHOR

Ben wrote this book. He lives in Minneapolis. He's married (sorry ladies). He refuses to share a photo of himself wearing a flannel shirt with mountains in the background, like every other author from 1985-Now.

18243282R00085

Made in the USA
Lexington, KY
23 October 2012